DATE DUE		
3/7/96			

COPING

WITH

School Age

Motherhood

Nancy Minor and Patricia Bradley

THE ROSEN PUBLISHING GROUP, INC./NEW YORK

Published in 1988 by The Rosen Publishing Group, Inc.
29 East 21st Street, New York, NY 10010

Copyright 1979, 1988 by Nancy Walsworth Minor and Patricia Bradley

Revised Edition 1988

Library of Congress Cataloging in Publication Data

Walsworth, Nancy.
  Coping with school age motherhood.

  1. Adolescent mothers—United States—Case studies.
2. Unmarried mothers—United States—Case studies.
3. Pregnant schoolgirls—United States—Case studies.
I. Bradley, Patricia, joint author.   II. Title.
HV700.5.W34   362.8′3′0973   78-14502
ISBN 0-8239-0923-9

Manufactured in the United States of America

Dedicated to our
school age
mothers, past,
present, and future

ABOUT THE AUTHORS ◇

NANCY MINOR, formerly NANCY WALSWORTH, is a native southern Californian and a graduate of the University of California, Santa Barbara. Having received a BA degree in Home Economics and a Secondary teaching credential, she accepted her first teaching assignment in a southern California coastal town. In her second year of teaching she became chairman of the Home Economics Department. Later she left her work to raise her two children.

During this period she became actively involved in the Junior League, devoting much of her energy to working with pregnant teenagers. When she resumed her career she accepted a position with Newport–Mesa Unified School District, where she designed and implemented an unusual school program for teenagers who had become pregnant and who often dropped out of their regular school.

Returning to the University of California, Irvine, she received a Counseling Credential. Later at the University of San Francisco she received an Administration and Supervision Credential and a Master's Degree.

Her marriage to John Minor added three grown children to her two, and a new interest in ocean sailing. Her other interests include sports, travel, and watercolor painting.

PATRICIA BRADLEY, also a native southern Californian, was raised and educated along the Pacific Coast from Newport Beach to Santa Barbara.

As a wife, mother of four, grandmother of seven, teacher, counselor, psychometrist, and educational psychologist, she has had many years of experience working with a variety of people's problems.

When she was promoted to the position of special education psychologist, one of the nine programs for which she became responsible was the School Age Mother Program. It was here that she met Nancy Minor, and it was the uniqueness of the S.A.M. Program that prompted the writing of *Coping with School Age Motherhood.*

Now retired, Patricia Bradley plays on a tennis team, actively enjoys writing, music, family, and friends, and works part time at Orange Coast College in psychological assessment.

Contents

Introduction

We have written this story in order to share with you our personal experiences, which could not have been known to many.

The book is based on the experiences of the girls, but in order for them to retain anonymity, we have obscured the true identity of each one.

Certainly the school setting was not a common one, nor were its participants.

Formal education and personal growth were to be achieved, but in such unusual ways.

Personal and family crisis was a reality for each girl.

The critical point in time was cried over, listened to, and discussed a step at a time. Was it to be enough?

CHAPTER 1

My S.A.M.

A s I drove down the tree-lined streets of our suburban community, a million thoughts were whirling in my head. They all centered around the fact that I was about to resume my teaching career after a seven-year absence. With an uneasy feeling in the pit of my stomach, and fleeting confidence, I turned onto the main thoroughfare and wondered about the task ahead. I knew I wouldn't have felt the degree of apprehension I now experienced if I were returning to my former position, but my new assignment would be be a totally different situation.

The traffic was heavy, with lots of cars turning toward small businesses and another stream surging toward the freeway. Housewives in car pools were gathering their flock. Children were pedaling along on bicycles, and a group of gray-haired people with shopping bags were waiting at the bus stop. But my mind remained elsewhere; what was in store for me—a thirty-five-year-old homemaker, mother, and now returning teacher, assigned to be the only instructor in a school for pregnant teenagers? What would it be like? What was adolescent pregnancy all about? How would these girls respond to a special school? What kind of girls were these? I even wondered what *I* might be like, once this unusual journey got under way.

I checked my scribbled directions twice before turning into a large well-worn parking lot. I pulled into one of the marked stalls and looked for a building I might recognize as a school. Across the wide expanse of asphalt, I spotted a small, insignificant-looking structure set apart from the rest. Painted a drab shade of green, the prefabricated metallic building looked like a miniature warehouse. From where I stood outside my car, I could see only two windows and a door. Could this be the educational home of the "School Age Mothers"? I walked slowly toward the building, and the faded letters "S.A.M." greeted me from their place on the door. I drew a deep breath and fumbled for the key. Finding it in the bottom of my purse, I took it out to wrestle it into the lock. I heard a faint click and, with a tug, pulled open the heavy door. With a flick of the light switch, I felt like "Dorothy in Oz": Everywhere I looked I saw warm, homey colors. Facing me across the room was a large orange and yellow couch, flanked on either side by easy chairs. A little shyly, I bounced on the edge of the couch as if testing a new piece of furniture at a department store. I sat just long enough to register the coffee table in front of me and an end table with a lamp on it to my left.

Venturing away from the couch a step or two, I noticed that the carpet still felt spongy under my feet. Everything was so perfectly new and clean! Even the faint aroma of fresh paint hung in the air.

On the wall directly across from the couch, I saw the familiar green chalkboard. What caught my eye were the words some considerate workman had left: "Welcome to SAM!" in bold letters. I felt a tingle of excitement as my

brain relished the confirmation: Yes, I was finally at
S.A.M.

Hurriedly, I resumed my exploring. I wanted to survey
the entire little school, which now seemed so totally re-
moved from its stark appearance from the parking lot.

To my right, adjoining the main room, a large kitchen
opened up, with light-blue, printed curtains above the
sink. I swept my hand across the counter tops, appreciating
their unused smoothness. There wasn't even a trace of a
crumb on the cutting board, and the shiny stove still had
cardboard around the oven door. The purr of the refrigerator sounded in the quiet of the room, and I almost left the
room without opening its bright yellow door. But my
curiosity got the better of me and I sneaked a peek! Unfortunately, there weren't any edible morsels. In fact, the
light sparkled on spotless chrome shelves and on the sides
of very empty drawers.

While I made my way out of the kitchen, I convinced my
stomach that it was only nervousness and not hunger causing the butterflies. The next few steps led me to the nursery. As soon as I poked my head through the door, a calm,
soothing sensation came over me. Everything in the room
seemed to yearn for the cooing, giggly sounds of young
children: the six cribs lining the walls; the sunlight playing
on the carpet through yellow and white gingham curtains;
the multicolored mobiles turning in the ever so slight
drafts of the room; music boxes; rattle toys; a changing
table and a rocking chair. I stood half-mesmerized in the
middle of the room, drinking in the atmosphere. For the
first time I could actually picture the precious babies that
would soon occupy those cribs.

After a few dreamy moments I returned to the main
room feeling less nervous than I had. But it suddenly occurred to me that I hadn't yet seen a teacher's desk or filing

cabinets. The only traditional school furnishings were the three long study tables next to me in the main room. So I went looking around again and sniffed out another room adjacent to the kitchen. It was a multipurpose room that I would call the crafts room. It had built-in formica tables along each wall. One table sported three seminew typewriters, and the other had sewing machines. There was one window in the room looking out on the back side of the parking lot in the direction of all the other buildings, and one bare wall that I decided would be the first subject for any redecorating. The vacant table in the center would be the place for future crafts projects.

I turned back to face the front door, undoubtedly looking a little puzzled as I'd still not found a place to settle with all my books and papers. Finally I realized that I'd been staring at the "office" door for the last few minutes. It was right next to the front door, so I had overlooked it when I came in and had since walked right by it at least twice.

Once inside my new office, I got to choose between the two desks there. I must have looked like a child trying to choose from a box of chocolates the one she most wanted —it was fun!! I finally chose the desk at the far end of the room. It faced the door and an interior window that looked out on the main room. I pulled out the executive-style chair behind my big oak desk, sat down, and allowed myself one long, reflective sigh.

The sound of a car door slamming outside jolted me to my senses. Then I heard a rustle on the front steps. From where I sat I could see the door slowly open. I jumped up to take one of the armloads the tall, slender woman tried to squeeze through the door.

"Hi," she bubbled enthusiastically, "I'm Michelle, your instructional aide."

"And I'm Cathy Whitfield," I responded. "It's good to have some company."

Before I could suggest that we set the boxes on the desk, Michelle's load was resting there, and she was rushing around to the various rooms, commenting on each, as I had done an hour earlier.

"Isn't this beautiful?" I heard her say from the kitchen as I set my box on the desk.

"I love it too," I said, "and I think the girls will be thrilled."

I followed Michelle into the nursery and watched her as she danced around the room, tapping the mobiles and shaking the rattles. She was probably twenty-five, with blue-green eyes and sandy blonde hair—almost the shade of my own, but hers was much longer. It served to remind me that I was in fact ten years older and would be carrying a heavier responsibility in the program. Still, I knew right then that this young woman who was quick to smile would be the perfect complement to my own slightly more sub-dued hopes for the S.A.M. school year.

Michaelle swept into the crafts room and, upon seeing the expanse of blank wall, commented, "Hey, a place to hang all the rock posters!"

We both laughed together, enjoying a lighter moment.

From the crafts room we returned to the office, where the stack of boxes waited to be unpacked.

"Well, let's see what you brought with you."

That kicked off an exuberant listing of things such as shelf paper, photographs, and book titles.

"Okay, let's get started," I said, her enthusiasm infecting me.

Michelle began cutting strips of paper and placing them in the kitchen cabinets. Talking as if we were old friends, I learned that she was single and liked bowling and raising dogs. While I clumsily tried to fit the paper to the drawers, she was trimming and cutting like a mowing machine.

We then brought in my cartons of papers and books and readied them for sorting and arranging. We had only this one day to prepare, as the regular school session began the next morning.

Out came file folders and Michelle put a heading on each one and stuffed papers into them. She then started on the books while I finished filling the second filing drawer. She mused over one of the titles before putting it on the shelf.

"Marriage, Contraception and Pregnancy—shouldn't it be the other way around?" she quipped.

I laughed.

It wasn't long before the boxes were empty, books were arranged neatly on the shelf, and the file cabinet looked as if we'd been there for years. It was such a relief to see the work completed that I kept silent when I double-checked the file and found papers under incorrect headings; I could fix that later. We both collapsed on the couch, pondering what the next morning would bring. We talked for a while and it was Michelle's question that hung heavily between us.

"What will they be like?"

"Well," I sighed, "I've lost a few nights' sleep wondering about that myself and, honestly, I don't know."

I had to mask my apprehension; the total responsibility of the school was on my shoulders—sink or swim. I continued:

"I'm sure everything will go fine."

"Yeah, Cathy, I think it will. We're in this thing together."

Michelle suddenly jumped up from the couch.

"It's almost five-thirty, and I'm pooped."

I looked down at my watch and couldn't believe it was that late. It was the first day and we had become so engrossed.

From the office Michelle called as she scooped up her purse, "I've got to go home and get ready for a hot date. I'll see you in the morning."

"Okay, Michelle. Thanks for all the help."

"Sure," she said, and was out the door.

I went into the office to gather up my own things and heard her old Ford rumble out of the parking lot. I walked back through the main room and headed for the door. I stopped there to take one last look at the words "Welcome to SAM" over my shoulder.

At 8:30 the following morning, Michelle and I found ourselves sitting at our desks in the office, listening, watching, and waiting for the school bus to arrive. The cups of hot coffee that Michelle brought in from the kitchen helped ease the tension.

The rumbling motor and the squeal of brakes alerted us. The big, bright-yellow bus had ground to a stop at the curb near the entrance of the parking lot. We jumped up and watched the girls disembark and exchanged "now or never" glances. Three were carrying babies and the others were in various stages of pregnancy, but all were so very young. The soft roundness of each little-girl face, some with braces, others with the carefree look of a tomboy, seemed a direct contrast to the pregnancy.

Michelle and I beckoned the girls in and, after smiles and greetings, they seemed to feel at ease. The girls were meeting one another for the first time, and conversations sprouted up about due dates and experiences related to their pregnancies. While I was busy with the paperwork of registering, out of the corner of my eye, I watched the girls wander around, just as Michelle and I had on our first visit.

As I had expected, all twelve girls expressed excitement and approval for their new school.

After an hour of informal chatter, I had the three mothers put their babies down for a nap so we could begin a more formal session of school. With unseen nervousness, I described for them the kinds of things we'd be doing. The S.A.M. program was designed to balance a formal classroom education with an education for their own special needs. I explained that we would also be learning about prenatal care, preparation for childbirth, and infant care. Most of them were pleased with the plan, and some looked almost relieved.

As I proceeded then to formally assign books and classes, I had a chance to hear comments the girls were making.

"Gee, your hair looks cute. Are you going to wear it that way Saturday when you go out with Bill?"

"Yeah, I thought I would."

"Do you want to double date?"

It struck me again how young they seemed and how oblivious they were to the responsibilities of their situation. Yet, even at their young age, they all would face or had faced the experience of giving birth to a child. Their personalities would unfold and their problems would become evident. I would need to learn how best to help them with the turmoil of adolescence and the miracle of motherhood.

With the preliminaries out of the way and the hours of the first day almost expired, a calm seemed to envelop all of us. The School Age Mothers were now assembled under the roof of the metal schoolhouse that I would soon call a second home because of my ever-growing involvement with my new family. (The girls, of course, did not reside at S.A.M. but came there only for the school day. Some girls lived with a boyfriend, some with an aunt and uncle, but the majority lived with their family.) The reality of my situation now registered in my brain, replacing all my visions and apprehensions. It was with this feeling of hope that the first day ended and my journey truly began.

CHAPTER 2

Julie

E ach morning when the bus arrived, the girls came into the office one by one to talk about their experiences. Soon the entire group congregated around my desk and were engrossed in conversations about boyfriends, parents, and babies. I enjoyed these informal talks because it was the time when we were best able to get to know one another. It was also the time when the group unity was strengthened and we became much like a very special family.

Once all the news had been shared, the group moved out into the main room to begin prenatal exercises and schoolwork. The rustling of papers and the sound of notebooks opening and closing gave me the cue that all were well on their way to a good study period. But this day, Julie remained behind. Normally a happy, thoughtful girl, she had a deeply distressed look on her fifteen-year-old face. We sat alone together and the tears began to well up in her big brown eyes.

"I don't know if I should keep my baby or give it up for adoption," she cried as she poured out her story.

Julie came from a loving, religious family who would

support her in any decision she might make regarding the baby. However, her mother was busily knitting baby things in anticipation of the coming event. Julie felt that her father was very loving and understanding but was interested most in her future. He would explore her possible directions as a mother caring for her child and as a college student studying nursing. In the evenings the family would sit around the dining-room table and have long talks, going over all the possible alternatives. Poor Julie's head was often spinning with so many thoughts and feelings that she seemed to burst and the tears would flow again. Should she keep her baby or give it up for adoption?

Her boyfriend also stood by her. They were both so young and had decided that at this point marriage was out of the question. They both had still to complete high school, and he too had plans for college. And yet, if marriage could be a solution, he had said that he would marry her.

They both realized that financially marriage would be difficult and that, even with a part-time job, they would have to rely on their parents for support; and his parents had said that if he got married now and spoiled his college plans he had just better forget about ever coming home again. He had got himself into the problem and it was up to him to get himself out.

There in the office, as Julie told her story, a pile of wet tissues collected around her. I wanted so desperately to give her a magic solution to all her problems. But I wasn't the one who could make her decision for her. It would have to come from her. She was the only one in the world who could make the final decision. But what I could do was to care and understand and listen as she worked things through in her own mind. I wished that I could simply assume the burden of this so young mother-to-be who seemed so devastated. Unknown to me, a deep need within Julie to communicate her innermost thoughts and feelings to the baby inside her prompted her to write secretly a series of letters.

November

Dear Baby,

I love you and never want you to leave me. I know you know how I feel. I love you so *very* much.

I went to the doctor for the first time today and he said that you are due in late March or early April. I haven't told your father yet but I hope he will understand. I want you to know that I love him and that I think he will be a great father. It's exciting and unreal that you are growing inside of me. Right now we are so close and dependent on each other.

If you are a girl, I think I'll name you Heather because it is a fragrant flower and I like natural and growing things. If you are a boy I'll name you after your father because I think he will be very proud of you. Baby, you'll always be a part of me and so will he.

God help me to be strong so that I will be able to make the right decisions for you.

I'd better go now—until later—I love you forever.

Julie, Mom

The S.A.M. Program had the services of a psychologist one hour a week or on call as needed. Grace Hartley, the psychologist, and I had chatted about the special needs of the S.A.M. girls and had decided that a discussion group once a week would give the girls a chance to leran some skills in dealing with problems and become more comfortable and aware of their worth as individuals as they were stimulated and encouraged to talk and to listen. If a girl needed special help, Grace could meet with her separately. Grace was in her late forties. The gray in her ebony hair reminded one of her years of experience in working with young people. She was a soft-spoken, gentle person who possessed a great warmth and empathy for teenagers.

It was Grace's day to come for the discussion group. I was anxious to share with her my experience with Julie. I had hoped that Grace could help fit some of the pieces together in Julie's situation.

Grace arrived and went into the crafts room where Julie was busily painting the first coat of shellac on a little keepsake box. The shirring sound of the sewing machine played in the background. Grace found an empty chair near Julie at the large table. After the uneasiness of a newcomer joining their group had passed, Julie commented, "I love to make things with my hands. I'm not very good at some of these things." Julie waved her hand across the table, indicating the different crafts.

"The little box you're working on is beautiful, Julie," Grace said. Julie invited Grace to paint a face on one of the little flat rocks. Somehow this didn't seem like a setting where Julie and Grace might do some real talking, but Grace began to paint happily and Julie chatted easily. Soon one girl after another joined in the conversation as she worked.

Before long, Julie was talking about her need to decide about keeping or giving up her baby. Grace turned to Marie, who had recently given birth and had relinquished her baby for adoption.

"Marie, how do you feel now about your situation?"

Julie began to listen intently. Here was a girl who had actually given her baby up, talking about her experience.

Another girl with her six-month-old baby entered the room. She put the baby on the floor with a cookie and pulled up a chair to listen. The sewing machine stopped, and the girl sitting there interjected.

"I could never have given my baby away. He was a part of me—even though I'm not married, I have found a way to keep him. He is our family's first grandchild and my parents love him."

Marie answered, "I just couldn't have kept my baby. It wouldn't have been fair to the baby, my parents, or me. It just would have been a pain for everyone. I have things to do and places to go before I'm ready to settle down, get married, and have a baby. I want to find myself first. I want my baby to grow up with a daddy."

Julie said, "When you decide to keep your baby, you will find a way to make it happy—everything can turn out all right."

Just then, the child sitting on the floor began to cry. The cookie he had been eating, now moistened with saliva, dribbled down him and, as he wiggled about, the wet cookie was ground deeper into his clothing and into the carpeting. Julie and Marie both looked down as he screamed and waited for his mother to come to his rescue.

Then Julie and Marie were deeper into conversation as they worked even more furiously on their projects.

"How would you feel if you were the child and your mother didn't want you and gave you up for adoption?" Julie queried.

Marie answered, "I did want my child and I loved him very much. I loved him so much that I gave him to a family that had both a mother and a father and the love to give a child that they couldn't have on their own. My child will feel that my loving and caring was the reason for his adoption."

Grace noticed tears standing in Julie's eyes and realized that her thoughts had now turned inward. There was a heavy silence in the room. Finally Julie said, "I don't know yet what I'm going to do, but I don't think I can give my baby away."

In the afternoon after everyone had gone home, Grace and I talked about the exchange between Julie and Marie. How could anyone gather her thoughts together in a room with crying babies and interruptions?

Grace needed to express her frustration about that noisy room, but she laughed at herself at the same time, for we both knew that a significant exchange had occurred in that very setting.

Grace saw Julie as a loving, giving girl with an unusually deep relationship with her unborn child. It was her capacity for loving and giving that probably had existed between her and her boyfriend, with the pregnancy resulting.

Here it was Friday, and the weekend ahead for Grace was one of quiet moments with Julie continually on her mind. She was caught up with the intensity of conflict in this young mother's mind. Who was she or anyone else to say what was right or wrong in any person's life? Yet, she knew that the passing of time and the reality of each girl's individual situation would dictate the rightness or wrongness of their decisions and their ability to cope with the circumstances.

Late November

Dear Baby,

Well, hello again—Guess what! It's Thanksgiving Day and believe it or not I have so much to be thankful for. I've changed a lot, not only physically but mentally also. I know now what I must do. I have definitely decided to give you up even though I really hate to, but I have to. It would be better for both of us.

Marie, a friend of mine at school, had a baby boy and she also gave him up. But, you see, I'm so young. I've got *so* much to do. Maybe one day you'll understand—maybe one day.

I love you and words could *never* say how I feel. Only God knows. It's so hard thinking I'll be without you that I have horrible nightmares. When I feel you kicking (which is a lot) I just want to hold you close. Maybe it would be easier if you weren't so active. Mom says that you are healthy and kick a lot like I did before I was born.

Most of all, I pray you get parents like mine. They're the greatest. I want you so much, to bring you up like I've dreamed of, to watch you grow, to hear you laugh, to see you smile, and to always be with you. It's so hard to be a mother at fifteen and to have to give you away—your own real, live baby. You are my baby and always will be—but not my "person" because you'll not be brought up by me. God help me if I'm wrong to do this but I don't really think I am. I could easily give you everything—everything but a father. Oh, why did this happen to me?

I feel, though, through me someone else's prayers will be answered. They will love you very much, maybe even more than natural parents because you are so *special* to them. Grow up loving them. I know how a mother feels toward her baby. If only people knew how very hard it is to give you up—it tears me apart.

Well, I'd better stop for now—Always love God and your parents and be good. I love you forever.

Julie, Mom

The weeks turned into months as Julie struggled back and forth with her decision. This once outgoing, giggly girl became more and more quiet. Now only occasionally would she cause the class to laugh at a joke or an antic. Her laughter was her escape from the depth of her struggle. I encouraged her smiles and was delighted when they turned into gay, happy sounds.

One morning as the girls were sitting on the couch, Julie began to examine her large stomach. She lifted her blouse to expose her bare skin and, as her fingers traced the slight bumps and recesses of her tummy, the girls speculated as to where the arms, legs, and body of this child lay. Julie would squeal as her child turned, and an arm or leg became very visible to the others. Soon others were comparing their stomachs, and there was much conjecture as to size, position, and sex of the unborn children.

Suddenly the front door opened and a maintenance man popped his head in. The girls screamed with embarrassment, and before he could say a word he decided he was in the wrong place and quickly ducked out. The laughter that followed was a needed release. By the time Grace arrived, everyone was in a good mood and eager to start.

The group began with everyone giggling and describing their embarrassment about the maintenance man's appearance. They were all in this frame of mind when Julie began to tell us about her long, struggled-over decision. The girls became silent as they looked at her face and listened as she told what she had decided to do about her baby. Tears filled her eyes as she spoke softly, "I'm going to give him up." The girls were stunned. But Marie understood, and she moved closer to Julie in her understanding. Grace, with tenderness and insight, set the stage for Julie to begin working through, out loud, the details of her decision.

"At first I was positive I was going to keep my baby," began Julie. "It is so terribly hard to give a *baby* to someone else—especially because it will always be your own. I will always be a mother even though my baby will belong to another family. I don't have a 'family,' a husband, and my baby needs the love of both parents. I want my baby to have the same chance in life that I had, with a dad and mom to love, trust, and respect. Not everyone is that lucky. I am fifteen. I look like fifteen, but I feel so much older. I think being pregnant made me grow up faster. I am only this baby's outside right now. Even though I have so much love to give, it hurts me that my baby won't know it." Julie looked down at her hands, then continued when her voice was steady again. "I am almost jealous of the love my baby will give its parents, but I'll manage because I know by deciding on adoption my baby can have a better life than a fifteen-year-old girl can give it."

Grace and I exchanged glances. Julie had more wisdom than many twice her age and maybe even more wisdom than some have in a lifetime. It just didn't seem fair that she should be going through all of this.

Even though the other girls had different opinions about adoption, they listened intently and thought through everything Julie had said, and they supported her in her decision. The group as a whole grew up a little just in that short time.

They were no longer high-school students, they were young adults with the profoundness of life's realities close at hand.

February

To My Little Baby,
  Hello again. It's past 11:00 P.M. but I had to write.
I went to the doctor today and heard your heartbeat.

You sound so beautiful. I just can't find the words to explain it. I love every minute of it just like I love it when you kick me. It feels so strange and so good. This morning I awoke before you. My mom started talking and all of a sudden you jumped and were awake too. It was an experience I'll never forget. For the first time I knew you were a whole different person.

Baby, I was just thinking about how it's going to be without you, in the hospital and afterwards. It's so confusing. I'll be happy but sad; be with friends again but alone; be anxious but tired; a new person but the same; sure but confused; an adult but a teenager; a mother but childless; one instead of two. I guess I could go on and on but, if there's one thing for sure, being pregnant is sure an emotional strain.

Baby, I hope they give you these letters so that you will always know that I love you. Be good to your parents and enjoy life.

Love, Mom

Julie began a period best described as the doldrums. She had made up her mind but couldn't completely live with her decision. She would feel guilty about giving the baby up and feel guilty about keeping it. She fluctuated between being happy and sad. I worried about her endurance and hoped that her burden wouldn't be too much for her. How much could one person take? I spent time after school listening again and again as she went over and over her thoughts. It took all the control that I could muster to keep from breaking down with her. I reflected her words and thoughts so that she could visualize her problems and maybe think through them more clearly. But working through her problems would have to take more time. Julie's resolve (if it came at all) needed much more time—maybe as much as double the lifetime she had lived thus far.

March

Dear Baby,

I felt that I had to write you. It's hard to believe that I have less than a month to be with you. I guess that's what makes it so hard. I never think of things like it'll be all over or I'll be able to see all my friends again. I always look at it as, I'll miss you. I'll be alone and I'll never feel or see my baby again. Oh Baby, I do love you so much. It really hurts so bad to give you up. It seems like, after this is over, I'll never have another tear left to cry because even now they seem to run dry. You or anyone else will never know how hard it is. I love and want you, but I can't ruin your life—it means so much to me.

Maybe I'm doing the wrong thing for my sake by giving you up. But that's not saying it's the wrong thing for you. I'm not a super religious person but I want you to know that you always have God behind you. When I'm down or alone I turn to God or read his Bible, then I know I've got at least one best friend. That's why I want you to be raised in a religious family so that you can know God too.

Right now you are kicking me and I just love it. It seems as though we have been together for years instead of almost nine months. I keep thinking, "What if I go into the hospital tonight." Then I think of seeing you, holding and talking to you for the first and last time. It's all becoming so real now but so hard to realize. A lot of people have told me that I won't be able to go through with the adoption, but I know that I must for your sake. Baby, it's not that I can't take care of you, because I know I can. It's because I can only give you a mother's love, not a father's love. You see, you are very wanted but I can't deprive you of the greatest gift of all, that of a father's love.

I have been having some light contractions all week; that's why I think that you soon will be born. God help me through the adoption, that's all I pray. Be good, Baby, and always respect life. It's not as easy as it sounds.

Love, Mom

At school Julie diligently kept up with her studies as well as faithfully doing her prenatal exercises. She looked so large and uncomfortable that I wondered how she could even move. She was very conscientious about each exercise as if she were doing everything in her power to make the birth easier for her baby.

She and her mother had gone through our prepared childbirth classes, and both were just marking time until Julie's labor began.

Her face showed the strain of the past months and she appeared so tired. I realized I was staring through the kitchen window as thoughts of Julie continued. She still blotted out her turmoil with occasional jokes and laughter. One minute she was a wise old lady and the next a giddy young girl. She was a picture of contrasts. She was feeling all the highs and lows of adolescence along with the added burden of her pregnancy.

One morning I suggested to Julie that we start an imaginary countdown to the day of her baby's birth. Julie agreed a countdown would be fun. Each day, with a red felt pen, Julie made a big X through the number. She was anxious for the birth to come, but she didn't want to be separated from her child. Adoption was her decision, but she didn't know if she could withstand it. Oh, Julie, I thought, please be strong—now you know what you will do—you have made your decision. It is now so hard to feel comfortable with it. Perhaps in these last days you will be able to weave the fine threads together. Each night I wait for your phone call saying that you have delivered, and each day passes with another one ahead. Your baby is waiting; you are waiting; your family is waiting; I am waiting; the girls are waiting—while the days pass on and on so slowly.

Late March

My Dear Baby,

I love you so *very very* much. I never thought we'd last this long. I know that you should be born any day. I am so very tired but I don't want you to leave me. Even still, I am not sure what I should do. I love and want you so much, Baby. I'm afraid I might not be able to give you away. I wish I knew.

Last night the house next door caught on fire and our house came so close to burning. I was so scared. Out of all the important things I have worth saving, I thought only of saving these letters to you and the baby clothes my mom made for you. They are really the most valuable things I have.

Baby, about you—I don't want to go to the hospital because I don't want to give you up. That is the last thing on earth I want to do. I feel so sad and confused, yet I know down deep what I should do. Just remember, Baby, whatever happens, I'll always love you even if you leave me soon. I'll always have you in my memories.

Love, Mom

Early April

To My Dear First Baby,

Lately I've been having a lot of strong contractions. I don't know how long I can take it. I feel like I could die. My backaches keep me awake at night and contractions all day. I just had another contraction. Oh, Baby, when will this be over? I am so tired and weak because I haven't slept or exercised in days. I feel like I'm going to die or something. I went to the doctor's today and he said it was false labor. My mom heard your heartbeat for the first time and she was so thrilled. It's so hard on my parents that I might give you up. They want you so much too. I can see the hurt in them both, Baby, and it even kills me more. I love you but I want you to have a good life. Today was my father's birthday. He almost was a grandfather.

I keep picturing you as a little child in grammar school with the other kids picking on you and saying things like your real mother gave you up because she didn't want you, or, whatever happened to your father? How come you don't look like your brothers and sisters? You see, Baby, I don't want you to go through that because of me. Tell me, what would you do if you were me? Sometimes life is so hard.

Love, Mom

The ringing of the telephone brought me out of a deep sleep. It was 2 A.M. I answered, struggling with my sleepy brain. The words, "Mrs. Whitfield? This is Julie's boyfriend, Steve," brought me quickly to my senses. "Julie just had her baby. Her mother was with her during her labor and she said that everything went just fine." I breathed a sigh of relief. "Julie and our beautiful baby boy are both doing fine. They are together now. . . She wanted me to call you right away. I hope you don't mind," he said.

"Of course I don't mind, Steve." I was so numb all I could stammer was, "Thanks so much for calling." I was thrilled that she came through her labor so easily.

When morning finally came and the first girls arrived at the school, I passed along the news. Everyone was so excited. When their animation settled I heard a whisper, "Is she going to give the baby up for adoption?" I could not answer because I did not know.

April—In the Hospital

Dear Baby,

Well, hello, little boy. I can't believe it. You're a boy—happy, happy birthday. I had you very easily because I really felt that you did everything. It is such a miracle—I'm still in great shock. You weigh 7 lb. and 12 oz., pretty great, huh? I'm so proud of us both. Really I am.

I don't think I'll see you again. I saw you after I had you for about a half hour and I know that you are healthy and normal so that satisfies my reason for seeing you. I know that if I saw you again it would really kill me, so you see it's better for me, I know, not to see you again. I hear you cry often but you're just a big healthy baby and I'm so very proud (even though it seems so unreal). You look like me, of course, but I think you look more like your father. I keep imagining how happy some adopting parents are going to be because you are so beautiful.

I watched you being born the whole time. Your head was just born and you began screaming your lungs out. I watched everything about you. It is such a beautiful day today—your birthday. I love you so much—life is so great. The second you were born I knew exactly what I must do. I had to give you up because you really deserve a lot more than I can give. A boy needs a father.

I feel great, just a little tired. Once in a while I feel like crying, but the more people I talk to about you, the easier it is for me to accept that I should give you up. I'm so proud of you and really love you so much. Baby, just have a beautiful life, be happy and *always* love your parents. God knows how important they are. That's all I ask. Maybe one day you'll be really proud also—a proud father.

> Goodbye, Baby
> (I'll love you always.)
> Mom

Julie came to school just two weeks after childbirth to visit and tell the girls about her experience. She sat in her place on the couch where she used to sit and examine her stomach. But she had no stomach now. She looked almost as if she had never been pregnant.

The girls gathered around waiting for her to speak. She told her birth story in great detail and their young eyes widened with each passing sentence. She gave them courage and confidence when she spoke so freely.

One girl asked about her baby, and Julie, with the warmth of a new mother, said that the baby was in a foster home temporarily, waiting to be placed with his parents. She often wondered,when she was at the market or going down the street, if the baby she saw was her own but then rebuffed herself for thinking such a thing. She described her emotions during the past two weeks as high and low. Her pregnancy almost seemed unreal now.It was almost as if she had never had a baby except for the pride that showed through her face when she thought of her boy. The miracle of creating life showed through her whole being; yet that was what was tearing her apart. The life she created was with another.

Her boyfriend stood beside her and was as tormented as she. It was his son too, yet, because they had decided they were too young for marriage, they could have no family together now—the baby would have a better chance with someone else. He hoped that his baby's family would provide everything that he couldn't right now.

It was Julie's last day at S.A.M. She was returning to her high school. I was saddened at the thought of her leaving. Good-byes were so hard; but I realized that it would be best for her to get away from pregnancy and babies so that she could forget.

She put her arm around me and I around her, and she thanked me over and over for being so understanding. I wouldn't tell her how painful it was for me to see her go and how I felt that a part of me was going with her. I couldn't show her my tears and I blinked them back frantically. I was the teacher, and teachers couldn't cry in front of their students. I didn't want to make it harder for her to leave. It was hard enough already. She was departing from the part of her life that she would never forget but would have to leave.

Sweet Julie, I watched you grow up each day before my eyes. How deeply I appreciated having known you and how involved I became even if it was only for a short time —it seemed almost like a lifetime. Good-bye, I know that your experiences here can only strengthen you. You are such a special person to me, and whatever the future brings, you are one who has profited by the past.

School had ended for this day, and I was able to stay at my desk all alone just thinking.

S.A.M. was empty and quiet. I put my head in my hands and leaned heavily on the desk before me and let the tears fall drop by drop onto the blotter. Out of the corner of a watery eye I noticed a blue envelope with my name on it stuck in the corner of the blotter. Inside it read,

> Joys too exquisite to last,
> Yet more exquisite when past...
> Life is filled with these.
>   Love ya lots,
>   Julie

On, my heart goes with you, Julie...Good-bye...

CHAPTER 3

Mauvine

I t seemed so different, so empty without Julie. I kept thinking about her and wondering how she was doing back at her regular high school. I had to tell myself often that I must not dwell any longer on Julie, as the rest of the girls needed my attention now.

Trying to focus my thoughts on the present, at last, I glanced through the big window in the office out into the room where the girls were working. I was struck by the many differences in their lives. For some of them life was a continuous struggle for even the barest necessities and basic gratifications. Fighting, stealing, manipulating authority were part and parcel of their existence. How I longed to have every one of "my" girls happy and changed for the better as a result of the S.A.M. Program. I didn't want to face the facts, the realities of the situations some of the girls talked about. I had eternal hope; I was an optimist. I found it much easier to let Grace work with girls like Mauvine. Much of what I knew and felt about Mauvine had come secondhand from Michelle and Grace. Still, I felt close to her and watched her progress eagerly.

Mauvine's entrance to the school, in the middle of a

morning, was announced by a loud, disrupting engine sounding outside the window. All of us in the office stood up to look out at a rusty, dented once gray-blue van that was pulling into the diagonal parking space outside the door. On the windows of the van were curtains made from a black and white material printed with long-haired nude women.

Out of the driver's seat sprang a burly, blue-jeaned, barefooted, bearded man. He ran his hands through his long curly hair as a grooming gesture while he waited for Mauvine to get out of the van. Smiling, they entered the room and, seeing us in the office, came directly there.

"Hi," I greeted them, "welcome to S.A.M." It was already obvious the girl belonged to our program.

"Hi," Mauvine responded, "they sent me over here from the Continuation High School, so I guess this is where I'm gonna be going. This is my boyfriend, Gil."

I introduced Michelle and the girls who were in the office. Both Gil and Mauvine seemed totally relaxed as they sat down and chatted with the group. Gil eyed all the girls in the room with great interest. I learned Mauvine was sixteen and Gil was twenty. Mauvine offered, "Me and Gil are living together with Gil's brother. I had to move out because the place where my mom and I lived was too small for three of us; and then with the baby coming," Mauvine added as she patted her stomach, "Gil had to sleep on the floor and I got the couch because of being pregnant. My mom has a king-size bed in the bedroom but she won't let any of us in her room."

"You must have been really crowded there," I responded. I learned later that Maurvine did all the housecleaning, laundry, shopping, and cooking for her mother, brother, and herself. So much responsibility at sixteen. How heavy the burden some children bear.

"How come you guys can't sleep in that big bed?" one of the girls asked Mauvine.

"Ha, you don't know my mom! She has friends over sometimes." That silenced the group.

Gil decided he'd be "movin' along," as he wanted to go see some of his friends. He said he'd pick Mauvine up after school. Mauvine got up and gave Gil a big kiss as he stood up to go. With a repeat of the grinding engine noise, Gil drove off.

The group broke up to go to their studies, and Michelle volunteered to fill Mauvine in on the day's activities. Mauvine seemed to take an immediate liking to Michelle, and throughout the months to come she would tell Michelle about all the wild happenings and problems that went on in her daily and nightly life.

Several times when we met in the group, Mauvine brought up her feeling of conflict about the usefulness of a guy like Gil "hanging around." He would get money from his mother because "he was too damned lazy to get off his ass and get a job," Mauvine said. She had to get the money from him for groceries, or he'd have it all spent on booze. When he got roaring drunk he "beat up" on Mauvine and was so "shitty" she couldn't stand him. Yet what was she to do? Her choice was to run him so as to get the most benefit out of him. After all, hadn't she had to take over and manage her mother in the same way? Mauvine had told Michelle about the night last winter when she was worried about her mom's not getting home. It was long after midnight and, although that wasn't an unusual time, her mom usually made it home, drunk as always, but somehow home and into her king-size bed. That night, however, Mauvine recalled getting up several times to see if her mom had made it. By morning, really worried, she went out the front door and found the car in the driveway and her mom

stone cold to the touch because of the extremely cold
night. Mauvine thought she was dead because she didn't
move when she shook her, but she was sleeping off her
"drunk" of the night before.

"God, I sure was glad to find her," Mauvine remarked.
She felt it was no time for her mom to give up, what with
her brother already in "Juvy." "I was lucky not to get put in
when I ripped off those clothes and things at K Mart,"
Mauvine went on. "They just put me on probation. I
haven't taken anything since then, but if I need something
really bad, maybe I'll have to."

Michelle told Mauvine, "Yeah, sure is hard to need
something bad and not have any way of getting it. Watch
out, though, because you don't want to end up in big
trouble. Maybe you can get a job after the baby comes,
then you'll have some money of your own."

"Hell, I gotta take care of the baby," was Mauvine's
reply.

"You're not thinking about giving the baby up for adoption then?" Michelle ventured.

"You gotta be kiddin'! Give *my* baby up to some fuckin'
couple who don't care nothing about it?"

I walked in on their conversation and heard Mauvine
say, "Well, they're not gettin' my baby!"

And so it was. Mauvine never changed her mind.

One morning Mauvine arrived at school supercharged
with excitement and in need of an attentive audience. It
seemed that the night before Gil's brother had gotten wind
of his girlfriend going out on him. She was at the apartment
they all shared when Joe walked in, boozed up and already
ranting. He and Sylvie had a big argument. Sylvie said to
hell with him, he didn't *own* her.

Enraged, Joe pulled a gun from a drawer in his bedroom
and shot Sylvie—not to kill her, of course, just to warn her.

The police were called, and so was an ambulance. (Mauvine was obviously heady with her on-stage appearance.) It was *she* who told the story to the police and answered all their questions. Gil had split when he heard the sirens.

Joe was handcuffed and taken to the police car, once again declaring his innocence. He had acted only out of his feeling for Sylvie.

A complete soap opera in one morning. This was a bonus for the group seated in the office. Every girl was spellbound. Soon after, Mauvine organized the kitchen detail and could be heard ordering the girls to "set the table; fix the salad or heat up the casserole." For all her bizarre life experiences, she was a good, efficient manager. The girls took to her well. She had a sense of humor and often had them laughing with her. She'd poke fun at Gil or some one of the many guys who hung around the apartment where she lived. When she outmaneuvered one of the guys, she would tell the story in such a funny way that the girls respected her "smartness" and sometimes asked her how to handle a problem of their own.

Mauvine *was* smart. I felt that if she'd had someone to encourage her in getting a formal education, she would have been able to learn well.

I was surprised one day to find that a girl I'd been trying to reassure about childbirth,which she feared irrationally, responded to Mauvine's taking over. Mauvy had been sitting in my office listening to the conversation when suddenly she walked over to the bookshelf and pulled the *Birth Atlas* out and sat down beside Ellen. In her own words and using all the correct terms, Mauvine matter-of-factly proceeded to educate Ellen.

"This is the placenta," Mauvine said as she pointed to the large plates. "This is what the baby looks like at this stage. See the little fingers and toes?

"Here is the cervix dilating to the right size, two to ten centimeters. This is called transition. This is where you push. Here's where you go to the delivery room."

With confidence and calmness, Mauvine gave Ellen the reassurance that she could do her part of the job just as well as anybody else "'cause there was nothin' to it once you understood." Mauvy had such a plain, understandable way about her. I felt grateful and close to her for the help she was able and always willing to give to the girls in the group.

Mauvine's due date seemed an endless eternity away for her. She became tired, discouraged, and quieter than I'd ever seen her. Michelle came to her rescue with pleasant chatter and exchanges that sometimes brought brief laughter again to Mauvine. One day Michelle asked about the tattoo on Mauvine's hand—the number 14. Mauvine said casually, "Oh, that's the year I lost my virginity."

When the due date passed and another week went by, Mauvine began staying at home. I made phone calls to check on how she was feeling, but they brought little response. Mauvine seemed rundown and alone. Then, one day, our faithful telephone brought news from Mauvine's older brother. He had been released from juvenile hall and had gone to Mauvine and stayed by her until her labor began. Gil took her and her brother to the hospital. Her brother stood by during her long labor, which was punctuated by frequent outbursts.

"Damn you, Gil, you bastard, for getting me into this. If you had to go through this you'd chicken out like you always do."

"Why in the hell don't the nurses do anything around here; all they know how to do is give you an enema!"

At the end of the long night, a baby boy was born.

When Mauvine returned to school with the baby, she had dark circles under her eyes and seemed tired and worried about the baby, who had some chest congestion.

I talked with Mauvine about what to do for the baby and how important it was to check with her doctor and to keep him warm. The baby recovered, and soon after Mauvine appeared to be her old self again. She came to my office one morning to say she and Gil had broken up and she was moving in with another friend. The hassle of "running Gil" was no longer worth it.

As Mauvine's struggles with finances, living arrangements, the baby, her mom, brother, and other guys came back into full play, Mauvine's attendance at S.A.M. was less and less frequent.

Often I saw her in various places in the community, traipsing around with baby Gil on her hip in one arm, and later on in a stroller, walking down the street on her way somewhere.

My heart aches for Mauvine who must continue to struggle because she hasn't enough opportunity or support to help her get farther. Yet I know she will keep working to make her world as good as it can possibly be for her and her baby, because that's the spirit of Mauvine.

CHAPTER 4

Alicia

I never knew, when the door opened, who might be coming in. Sometimes it was a new student, often aimless and unwanted, who eventually found her way to our doorstep. This morning when I looked up at the sound of the door opening, I saw a hesitant look on the face of the girl who stepped inside. Seconds later, this fragile pale girl, with a frightened lost look in her eyes, stood before my desk.

"Is this the S.A.M. school?" she asked.

"Yes, it sure is," I answered, smiling the warmest greeting I could.

Her voice quivered as she spoke softly. "I'm Alicia and would like to enroll. My baby is due in four months. I am seventeen and would still like to finish high school."

With reassurance I told her, "You are in exactly the right place!" I welcomed her with open arms. "You don't have to go any farther, you have found us."

I reached for a folder full of admitting papers. "You don't have to worry about these papers now, just bring them with you when you want to begin," I said.

"Oh, I want to start right away," she explained. "I have nowhere else to go. I want to start now."

I took Alicia into the main room to introduce her to the group studying there, and then over to the couch where several other girls were knitting.

A new girl to the class was like a trespasser invading private property, but I was always pleased when the girls showed such special consideration. They made Alicia feel so welcome. We peeked into the nursery at the babies and Alicia asked, "Can I bring my baby here after it is born?"

"Oh, yes," I assured her, recognizing that she had decided to keep her child.

All the girls started at S.A.M. as strangers, and they understood how a new one felt during her first week—a little scared and strange, hardly believing she was really welcome and could belong.

That first week everyone made a special effort to see that Alicia was included in all the activities of the classroom. She helped with the cooking at lunch and took a turn with the babies in the nursery, but Alicia was still very shy and quiet.

Because of her extreme shyness, I was surprised when she showed an interest in unfolding her story to me.

One day we sat alone together where the others couldn't hear, and she began to talk about her past.

She had been living with her boyfriend. Alicia fumbled in her purse to get some pictures of him. She handed her favorite to me and said, "That is Don." As I studied the glossy photograph, she described him as being very kind and considerate. I couldn't help but notice in the picture that his hair was graying at the temples and he appeared to be in his early forties. She said that Don had always liked younger girls and had been married when they had first met. He divorced his wife, and Alicia and Don took an apartment together.

The next photograph showed the two of them. Don was standing very tall and distinguished, with frail, thin Alicia clutching his arm. What a contrast between the two of them. It was not only the twenty-four years that separated their ages, but his strength and her weakness that showed through vividly. When she realized that I wasn't going to criticize him, only accept him, she seemed to relax all over.

In a soft voice Alicia said, "Three months ago Don committed suicide. He shot himself in the head."

Trying not to show my sudden shock, I felt the photographs get hot in my hands. I held them now at the corners so that my perspiring hands wouldn't stick to their shiny surfaces. I swallowed hard, trying not to gasp as I murmured, "I'm so very sorry."

In a broken sobbing voice she said, "He didn't even know he was going to be a father. I couldn't stand it—I mean being separated from him—so I took every pill I could find. I didn't want to live either." She continued, "I woke up in a hospital room with doctors all around my bed. I didn't want to wake up. I wanted to forget everything."

"When I was well enough, they transferred me to a psychiatric ward and then the shrinks started working on me." Alicia now talked in quiet, measured tones, looking directly at me as she spoke. "I hated the place. I wanted to get out so badly. The only thing good about the place was that it was there I found out that I was pregnant. I'm carrying the only thing left that is truly Don's—his baby. I want this baby so badly."

"All of us here want you, Alicia, you are a very special person. I'm so glad you have come," I reassured her.

As Alicia became even more comfortable at S.A.M. she told her story to some of the girls, and soon all knew of her trauma and rallied to help her in any way they could. They realized how important it was for her now to lean on us, and they became like part of her family.

It was Friday and the group assembled around the couch in anticipation of Grace's arrival. Michelle was watching the babies so that we could have uninterrupted time together. Many different conversations sprouted up regarding the topic for the day—"Parents." The girls had decided that for sure they wanted to vent their feelings about parents, and they looked anxiously at the door for Grace.

Alicia joined the group and sat silently with a blank stare. At last Grace bustled in with her purse balanced on her notebook and glasses case in hand.

"Hi, everyone! I got the word that you have been wanting to talk about parents. Is it you as parents or is it your parents that you want to talk about?" Grace asked.

Well, the girls actually hadn't thought about themselves as parents like their own parents. So we began by talking about their parents and the way they did things, and then the girls discussed ideas and feelings about parenting. During the peak of this animated discussion I noticed that Alicia's chair was empty. I hadn't seen her leave. Where could she be?

I slipped away to find her in the restroom blowing her nose with toilet paper. She was very upset. We sat down together on the bed in the room there, and she told me that her mother was divorced and was never around much. She and her brothers more or less took care of themselves. And when she was in the hospital, her mother had moved away, leaving her to come home to an aunt's house. She certainly didn't want to be that kind of a parent. In fact, she felt that being so nervous, she didn't even know if she could be a good parent at all! She thought maybe she would give the baby up for adoption and then she wouldn't have to worry about being a parent. It took a long time to calm Alicia and reassure her again of her worth and her baby's need for her.

Alicia's baby kicked or turned just then, as if reminding her of its presence. She gave a startled jump and commented that the baby's movement surprised her. It was a good happening though, for Alicia seemed to regain some confidence and composure.

Grace and Alicia got together for a conference, but Alicia regarded Grace as "just another shrink" and would only say what she thought Grace wanted to hear. It was frustrating for Grace, I'm sure, when she told me, "Cathy, it will have to be you who helps Alicia, as she can accept your support." I realized then that I was going to be the one person wholeheartedly involved with Alicia at this time. Each day I offered refuge for Alicia. I waited and waited for a smile or any indication that her pain was easing. Twice this day she smiled and I felt well rewarded. When she spoke quietly with another girl I was very pleased. Alicia's progress went ever so slowly, but, oh, I *was* seeing progress. Our casual conversations were always initiated by her. She wanted to see if she could trust me and in time found that she could.

Alicia was taking an American History class and joined the girls who had planned for the lecture and discussion today based on the preliminaries to the Civil War. As the students role-played people in the North and South, I felt Alicia's eyes upon me. She was a million miles away. I would look up only to see her turn away. She seemed anxiously wanting to say something. I waited to see what would happen. The others continued in a heated debate, and our discussion lasted almost an hour. Alicia remained lost in her own world. I wondered how long she could wait before spilling over.

Our eyes met, and the glance seemed to mean we would communicate further.

The group closed their books and gathered their notes together. I felt a soft tap on my shoulder. "Mrs. Whitfield, may I talk with you?" Alicia asked quietly.

We went into the office. It was like a dam bursting as Alicia's words began tumbling out.

"I'm so worried about my baby. It probably will be born all deformed for what I've done to it—like taking all those pills when I was first pregnant. I am borderline diabetic and Rh-negative too. This baby has three strikes against it already, and it isn't even born yet. It has been haunting me, too, that both Don and I used pot and cocaine. This baby might be born a blob or something. It scares me so much. The baby is all I have left of Don, and now I want it so badly. It kills me that I might have harmed it. It's all I have, and it seems to me that even it won't turn out right. I'm so depressed and nervous, I just want to reach for the pills and forget it all." She cried and cried.

I put my arm around her and it seemed to calm her ever so slightly. I felt she was uncomfortable with motherly affection. What could I do? How could I help Alicia? I was crying out for help and had only myself. I kept thinking, I'm just a teacher and I don't have the training and experience for this sort of situation. I would have to get my thoughts together quickly, as Alicia needed help right now —a referral might be too late. I would have to rely on myself. Carefully I started.

"Alicia, you are so special to me. I really do care what happens to you. Each day I look forward to your coming, and in the evenings I think of all the things we have talked about these past months. I have gotten to know you so well, and I know what it takes to make it through this. Trust me when I say that you have what you need. I know things are terribly hard right now, but remember that whenever you feel down we can always talk—day or night."

Alicia appeared to feet better and, after gathering herself together, she joined the others. I sat quietly a few moments wondering about it all. Had I said or done the best thing for her? I didn't know. Sometime later I called our school nurse and asked her to find out as much as she could about the studies of drugs effects on the unborn child. I would talk to Alicia later about the importance of telling her doctor in detail everything regarding the kinds and amounts of drugs, and when they were taken.

Most important, I called Grace. I needed her help and support. If this girl didn't make it, her baby certainly would be lost with her. Grace advised me to remain in close contact with Alicia, listening for her feelings and continuously giving her the support she needed. Grace assured me that Alicia's trust in me and in herself would grow as time went on.

During the month that passed, Alicia and I had many long talks. I always let her take the initiative, and our conversations were varied. It was when she said, "I must make plans for my baby's birth and get everything ready," that I realized the worst had passed. "I want my baby to have the kind of life that I never had—to go on picnics and have fun; it deserves a childhood. We will do things together. We will have each other," she explained with the exalted anticipation of a happy mother-to-be. I hoped her happiness would continue, and it seemed to for weeks.

One morning in the office, when the girls were sharing their recent activities as they liked to do, Alicia told us about her latest visit to the doctor. He had wanted to do some tests. She revealed her large abdomen. At the lower right and left were needle holes. Four holes on the right and five on the left. The doctor was trying to extract some of the amniotic fluid for testing but wasn't successful and kept trying again and again. She was to return later for additional tests. Other than being uncomfortable during the tests, Alicia seemed to come through these procedures in fine shape emotionally. But I was very concerned. The amniotic fluid was not tested unless there was a concern about a deformity of the baby. I masked my emotion. I had been so terribly anxious about the health of the baby, and this testing certainly was not good news at all. But the matter was between Alicia and her doctor, and I would stay out of it. She was receiving good medical care, and that was my primary concern.

Because of this recent news, the final weeks before her baby's birth were filled with apprehension for me. Frail Alicia couldn't take any more tragedy in her young life, and at this point I wondered how much more I could take in my life working with these girls. I *must* remain strong. I wasn't going to be a liability. I loved my work and just had to keep believing that all things had a way of working out.

It often took more strength than I thought I had to continue each day being Alicia's strength too.

I must have covered my feelings well, though, because as her due date approached the girls made jokes in giddy expectation. It was so good for Alicia. Each afternoon as she left they would say, "We probably won't see you tomorrow," or, "Call us from the hospital." Alicia loved the attention and seemed to thrive on it.

The following day Alicia didn't get off the school bus. "She's in the hospital," the girls said as they burst through the door. "When the bus went by her house this morning, her aunt said that she had gone into the hospital at 4 A.M."

"Do you think she has delivered?" Julie asked.

"How many think she is having a girl? How many a boy?" Michelle carefully tallied the votes on her steno pad: ten for a boy and four for a girl. I always encouraged their games on "birth" days because it provided the relief we all needed.

Every time the telephone rang, all eyes were on Michelle as she answered, "S.A.M. Program." Was it Alicia? Was it her aunt? No, just a call from one of the high schools. The phone seemed to ring so many times, and each time there was a hush of anticipation. No matter how important the call was, none was as important as *the* call we all waited for. "Maybe somehow we could call her," someone suggested.

Classes were given as usual, Science, Math, English. No one seemed able to concentrate.

At 1 P.M., after it seemed like the one hundredth call, Michelle said, "It's Alicia's aunt. She has had the baby!" We all gathered around the extension phone as if in a football huddle.

"Alicia is just fine and she had a beautiful little girl. Everything is perfect. The baby weighed 6 lb. 8 oz. and is 19 inches long," the aunt reported.

"How long was her labor?" Michelle asked.

"Fourteen hours. She had a very normal birth."

I breathed a sigh of relief—everything was *normal*. I immediately put out of my head as forgotten the words I'd planned to say if things hadn't been all right.

Michelle referred back to her steno pad and said, with teasing authority, "The four girls who guessed 'girl' don't have to do the dishes for a week." "Hoorays" from the winning side and "Boos" from the losing side became laughter as both sides realized how hilariously they were acting. I leaned back in my chair and laughed. My exhilaration vented the concern that had pressed so heavily upon me these past four months. Hooray for Alicia! Hooray for the new baby!

CHAPTER 5

Joe

This morning, as usual, I spent time with many of the girls individually, sitting down beside each one and answering questions and piquing their interest. I was going over an English lesson with Anne when the front door opened. Everyone raised their eyes to greet the couple entering. "Maybe a new student," Anne wondered, as I stood up to meet them. "Is this the S.A.M. school?" the girl queried. "Yes, it is, I'm Mrs. Whitfield."

"Oh, good. The counselor from my high school sent us over. I'm Rita and this is Joe." As I ushered them into the office, I could feel the anticipation of the girls at the possibility of having a new student.

Joe was a tall lanky unfinished man who looked younger than his 17 years. His cheeks were smooth, with barely a hint of a beard. His black shiny hair cascaded over his forehead, and from time to time he shook it back nervously. He seemed protective of Rita and sat close by her as he began the conversation by talking about their baby. Rita was very quiet. Her eyes were downcast a great deal of the time. I explained how the school was run, with each girl taking classes individually, and how the students were from different schools and in different grades. S.A.M. was like an old one-room school where many things were going on at the same time. And teasingly I said that she was stuck with only one teacher—me!

That brought her eyes up and a smile to her lips, allowing a row of braces to become visible. Rita's arms covered her stomach in the characteristic posture carried over from the embarrassment and trials of the regular school. Even in today's modern society, girls continued to be harassed by unkind remarks made by their peers. She looked as though she had been uncomfortable for a long time at school. Her black hair was well groomed, and her face, scrubbed shiny, showed traces of adolescent acne.

"Joe and I have been going together for a long time," Rita finally spoke, but softly. "We wanted to get married, but my mother won't let us. She won't even let Joe come over to the house anymore." Joe broke in, "Rita's parents are so unfair. They make her do all the work just because she's the oldest. It's just not right. I've tried to do everything I can to help her, but her parents don't like me and won't give me a chance."

"It's only when we're out like this that we get to see each other," Rita added. "It's almost like I'm trapped. My parents say they are ashamed of me and don't want me out where everyone can see me. So, after school I must go home and not go out of the house until the next day. My Mom has a list of things that I have to do before she gets home from work. If she isn't satisfied with what I do, she gives it to me across the face. I can't stand it around the house. My father is just the same, only he slaps harder."

Joe's eyes pleaded for help. He wanted to take Rita away from her family and make a home for the two of them, but he had no money, no job, and no authority with Rita's family. He lived with his sister and her husband, and they didn't want Rita moving in with them.

I introduced Joe and Rita to the girls at S.A.M. and showed them through the tiny school. They wanted to stay for the morning and found a comfortable place on the couch. I gave Joe a book on prenatal development, and the pictures of the unborn babies fascinated him. Soon his arm slipped around Rita's shoulders, and they shared dreams about their unborn child. They were oblivious to everyone. I looked closely at this boy-man; his untamed eyes gave no clue as to whether he was aware of what was ahead or had ever given it serious thought. The scene before me was one of quiet togetherness.

A car slamming on its brakes out in front caused Joe to jump up. "That's my brother. He's picking us up. If Rita wants to come here to school, when can she start?" he asked.

"She can come tomorrow if that's not too soon," I answered.

"We'll be back tomorrow," Joe called over his shoulder.

Rita began her classes the next day, with Joe by her side. I didn't ask Joe if he should have been in school or working or what? I let him be. His presence indicated to me that for now he needed to be at S.A.M. I wished I could have enrolled him. He was a "S.A.M. student" if there ever was one, but he was male.

Joe worked with Rita during the study period and participated during class discussion. After a few days the girls became comfortable with Joe there and accepted him without question. He was now a part of the S.A.M. family.

His presence added a new dimension to our otherwise all-girl school. He was devoted to Rita and she to him. He was open to express his ideas and did so from time to time. He didn't interfere with or prove in any other way to be distracting to the other girls.

On Grace's day, Rita sat in one of the upholstered chairs while Joe took a chair by the study tables off to the side. Grace started with an invitation for Joe to join the group and, if he wanted to, tell how his week had gone with the rest of the students. Joe moved his chair awkwardly toward the circle. He had a shy expression on his face. Grace recognized that he wanted to be a part of the group but was not yet ready to speak. She moved smoothly along to the girl on his left, who was anxious to begin. Both Rita and Joe participated very little. Grace knew they needed time to feel comfortable with the group. This nonthreatening approach reassured them both. When they were ready to participate, they would.

The next week Joe's chair was in the circle beside Rita's. The girls were talking about handling emotions, Grace's topic for the day. Several times Joe was about to speak. Finally he burst out. "I get so mad at Rita's parents that I want to go over and punch them out. They are making it so hard on us."

Rita interrupted, "Joe, if you came to the front door you know what my dad would do—Mom too. How do you think I feel? I don't like it either."

Joe continued, "It makes me all sick inside when I think of the baby being raised like this with us apart and with your parents. I always wanted my children to have the things I couldn't have. It was gonna be different for them. Can you see now, Rita, why I'm so mad? Your parents are taking everything away from us."

"I know Joe, but what can I do? I'm so unhappy and confused."

Quietly Grace began, "It *is* confusing and does make you

feel angry and sad, but we have to remember that there are so many difficult things to work out when two people are young, as you are, and need to finish school and get some kind of training for a job that will pay enough money to support a home, and a baby. When parents are against a couple's getting married and are unwilling to provide help, it's especially difficult.

"We have to start thinking about the things you can do now that will help you get what you want later on."

Anne chimed in, "Yeah, like me. I have to take care of my sister's baby all afternoon and do the housework so she'll take care of my baby so I can work at Taco Treat in the evening. I'd like to have my own place, but I don't have the money." Joe and Rita listened seriously as if realizing what huge obstacles they had to face.

Little by little as the weeks went by, Grace and the rest of the group talked about decisions, priorities, choices. All the while Joe seemed to be thinking, growing, and learning.

The routines of school took over with Rita's questions unanswered. The daily work periods sometimes were broken only by the sounds of lunch being started. It was a time of schoolwork production and learning. Guest speakers came from time to time to talk about parenting or birth control or adoption. Joe and Rita enrolled in a prepared childbirth class.

Weeks became months. They slipped quietly into what Grace and I liked to call the "waiting period." It was a time of slow, quiet change. There were the physical changes of pregnancy that Rita was experiencing. Her tummy became large and rounded. She would take Joe's hand and put it on the place where she felt movements. Joe would smile with delight as he felt the ripples of an arm or leg glide past his fingers.

There were the emotional changes of the waiting period, which meant the clarification of Joe's and Rita's personal feelings and the strengthening of their relationship. Mentally they were looking ahead, planning, making decisions, solving problems, and learning the importance of communication. So much was going on inside of Joe and Rita, but on the surface everything seemed quiet. They were preoccupied. The months went by.

Joe dropped out of regular school and began night school. It was a better solution for him because he was spending so much time at S.A.M. He typified the student who had to feel good about himself before he could learn. It was Grace's and my feeling that personal worth must exist first before academic success can occur. Joe was a perfect example. He was beginning to feel like a worthwhile person, and he had made some positive changes. He talked to Michelle about jobs. She was an expert in finding jobs for everyone. In a flash she had the local paper in hand and was circling the ads that appealed to Joe. Then she prepared a "telephone talk" so that Joe would know what to say when he called for an appointment. With bus schedule in hand, Michelle mapped out a route and times for him so he could begin making appointments. She told him not to be disappointed but to continue, and when this list was exhausted she would go on to another.

He made the calls in the office. After each one he would ask Michelle, "How'd I do this time?" "Every time is better, Joe; you are getting to be an expert."

Joe got his job. A ball-point pen factory in town hired him to fit casings over the ink cartridges. He would receive the minimum wage, but pay increases were promised after he was experienced. He came by school on his first day, partly to say good-bye and partly to have us bolster his confidence. He vowed to make enough money to marry

Rita and take her away from her parents and make a home for the two of them.

The girls all said good-bye. Rita kissed him "good luck," and off he went to his first day on the job.

Rita's due date was approaching and both she and Joe were excitedly anticipating their child's birthday (as they liked to call it). Joe's job was working out fine, and in another month he would be receiving his first pay raise. Rita's parents, however, continued to be an immense problem to her. Nothing had changed. They were rigid and locked into their position. Joe would not be a part of Rita's life.

This morning as I watched the girls get off the bus, I couldn't help but notice Rita's painful expression. The other girls were helping her as she slowly walked from the curb to the back of the parking lot to S.A.M.'s door. As the door opened one of the girls announced excitedly, "Rita's in labor; we were timing her contractions, and they are 10 minutes apart. She had two on the bus." Rita wanted to lie down.

She moved slowly to the bed and sank down on the brightly colored spread. With the beginning of another contraction she took a "cleansing breath" and began slow abdominal breathing. As I looked at Rita laboring there, I thought of how much it must have taken for her to make it to school. How had she covered up her signs of labor so her parents wouldn't trap her at home? How had she waited on the corner for the bus—cars rushing by and no one knowing she was in labor? How had she endured the bus ride with all its bumps and ruts and wide turns, clutching the metal bar on the back of the seat in front of her, holding on as she perched herself on the hard black seat feeling every inch of the road? Rita's contraction ended, and she turned her wide dark brown eyes to me. "Call Joe for me, please, Mrs. Whitfield; he doesn't know."

"I will—right away. Does your doctor know?"

"No one knows but us. Would you call the doctor too?" she added.

"Don't worry about anything," I assured her. "Everything will be O.K."

Joe was very anxious and excited when he heard the news. He would get over to school as soon as he could even if it meant he had to steal a car. "Oh, don't do that!" I said, reacting seriously to his joke.

"Aw, you know I was just kidding, Mrs. Whitfield. Tell Rita that I'll be there soon."

"Okay, I will. Goodby, Joe."

My next call was to the doctor. I was told to call back when Rita's contractions were steady at 5 minutes apart. I returned to Rita. "Mrs. Whitfield, they're 7 minutes now!" All the girls surrounded the bed. I felt that Rita should have some breathing room, and they agreed. They moved from the room back to their seats and to their work. But no matter what the girls attempted to do, they were preoccupied with Rita's labor. So was I.

Joe arrived out of breath. He had taken a bus and had run the rest of the way. "Where is she?" he asked breathlessly. We went to her. They caressed each other. I noticed tears in Rita's eyes. I closed the door so that they could be alone, knowing that they needed this precious time together.

We went through the motions of the day not really totally involved.

Joe emerged and announced that Rita's contractions had been 5 minutes apart for about half an hour. He called the doctor, using such a grown-up manner. Michelle and I exchanged glances. The "telephone talks" had really helped.

"The doctor said that we should be getting to the hospital," Joe reported. "But before we go I'll leave a message at Rita's mother's job telling her where we are going. Rita can talk to them afterwards."

I offered to take them as soon as I could arrange for someone to watch the class. "Would that be O.K.?"

"Sure," he answered confidently. He returned to Rita.

It wasn't long before we were in the car on the way to the hospital. Rita was doing fine. It was I who was nervous—trying to act calm. We seemed to catch all the red signals, and cars seemed to be turning in my way as I drove carefully as I could down the main boulevard. With relief I turned in at the hospital.

They got out at the front entrance and turned to thank me. I shall never forget the picture they made as they walked slowly through the door. Joe, still shaking the hair from his eyes, had his arm around Rita's shoulders. He looked too serious and too controlled to be seventeen and a half. Rita was totally involved with her labor. She was prepared and on top of her contractions. But she too looked out of character. Her round face smiled a thank-you through her braces. With a last wave, the door closed behind them. I sighed a deep sigh, turned the car around, and headed back to school.

Later that evening, Joe called at home to tell me that they had just had a baby boy. He had been with Rita throughout her labor and had witnessed the birth of his baby beside her. Joe recounted his experience.

"At first it was simple. Rita and I talked and kidded around. The nurse checked her and she had dilated to 3 centimeters. It sure didn't seem like much progress for all her labor so far. The doctor came in and broke the water. That really made her contractions stronger and closer together. Her back was hurting her, so I rubbed it to make it easier. Rita needed me to help her and talk to her. She calmed down when I kept telling her that she was doing a great job. She was especially able to relax when I rubbed her shoulders and neck. I timed her contractions just like we had practiced in class. I kept saying how much I loved her. She liked that and then allowed the contractions to work for her, not against her. The doctor checked her again and she was up to 5 centimeters. It seemed like we would never make it to 10. It was taking so much out of her—she was working so hard, and now even my back was killing me from bending over her for so many hours. I finally sat down on a chair beside her. Contraction after contraction, Rita labored on and on. She began to get cranky and to have the urge to push. Could we be at 10 at last? I called the nurse to check her and it was good news. She was at 10!

"With the next contraction she held onto her knees, leaned forward, took a deep breath, and pushed. It was just like we practiced. I counted so that she would hear me and have a big long push. She took another breath and pushed again. Her face turned purple and was all wrinkled up. Her eyes were closed tight. At first I thought something was wrong with her. I wondered if it needed all that pushing to get the baby out? Rita told me that the pushing felt good to her. It was hard for me to believe, but I began to believe her when she smiled between contractions. The baby's head was crowning. I saw it. I called the nurse and the next thing I knew they had rolled her bed to the delivery room and I was wearing green clothes, a cap, and a funny mask. I had to say 'Rita, it's me' before she recognized me.

"Rita was on the delivery table, and the doctor fixed the mirror so that we could see. I saw a little bit of the baby's head. It looked like he had black hair. There was lots and lots of pushing. I kept saying how good she was doing. We looked up at the mirror, and I saw the baby's whole head —ears and all. His eyes were closed. Another big push and out came the body. The doctor held him up and we heard

him cry! 'Our son! Our son!' we shouted together. I put my
head down by Rita's and we both cried together. What a
miracle it was! I shall never forget it. The baby was brought
to us, and Rita nursed him right away. I touched his wet
black hair. It was long and fine. I felt how warm he was.
Our son. Joseph Jr. I could never have believed it if I
hadn't been there. I put my arm around them both, and
Rita smiled the warmest, calmest smile I had ever seen. It
was beautiful."

Choked with emotion and unable to go on, he said good-
bye softly. I found my eyes were full of emotion too.

Joe kept us informed about Rita's recovery. He had held
his baby at the hospital, but the few short days there were
over and Rita was back at home. He became the outsider
again. Rita's parents still believed that he was too young
(not even graduated yet, they would say), and they wanted
more for their daughter than he could offer. A feeling deep
inside Joe began to overtake him. He felt a sense of ur-
gency to take Rita away and establish for them both the
kind of home he so desperately wanted for his child. But
where could he go? He hadn't saved enough money to
support her. More and more the feeling welled inside him.
He couldn't take it anymore, and he made a plan. He had a
married cousin who lived in a distant city. He could arrange for Rita and the baby to stay with them until he made
more money and could join them. Her parents wouldn't
follow her there, and she would be safe. He checked the
bus schedule. It was a 10-hour trip, and he had the money
to buy the ticket.

When Joe told her about his plan, Rita was troubled. She
had always obeyed her parents even when she thought
they were wrong. It was a big step for her. She needed
time to think about it. It was a big change for her to go from
overprotection to freedom and to change from being her

parents' child to becoming a mother herself. Her decision became clearer as her mother began to take over the rearing of little Joseph. The baby in the house added a competition between the two mothers. Rita realized that Joseph was going to be raised by her mother as she had been, and she couldn't stand the thought of it. Being unable to confront her mother, she went to Joe and confided in him. She was ready to leave home. The next day while her parents were at work, they packed her clothes. The large cardboard box strained against the cord tied around it as Joe carried it to his brother's car. Rita was scared about her parents' finding out, and they had to move quickly. Everything was so strange. She wanted to go, but she was afraid. Joe's brother dropped them off at the bus station by the freeway. They sat huddled together on the bench outside. They clutched one another in an unending embrace. The tears streamed down their faces and mingled as they pressed their cheeks together. Rita sobbed uncontrollably. Joe's slender arms encompassed her and the baby as he rocked them both gently. They sat there unable to speak. In the distance, the roar of the bus was heard. The inevitable became reality in an unreal way. The bus approached, but it was like a dream. Joe and Rita were unaware of the other passengers as they lined up. Joe stroked the baby's head and kissed him on the forehead. He reached into his back pocket for the ticket and an envelope that held the money he had saved. He put it into Rita's hand as the bus door squeaked open. The other passengers boarded. Joe and Rita stood up weakly, and as if in a trance moved toward the door. They kissed their last kiss, and Rita stepped up onto the bus stairs. She moved along the aisle and sat down by the window, waving little Joseph's hand. Joe touched his lips with his fingers gesturing his good-bye. Rita was overcome with grief.

Joe came by school the next day to tell me about Rita's going. It didn't surprise me that things had taken this turn. It pointed out to me how desperate they both had become.

I never saw Rita again. But from time to time Joe stopped by to talk and share some of his experiences.

His days were long and empty without Rita. He was tormented with loneliness. The present was unbearable agony. He lived for the future. The slow passage of needed time was filled with the grief of their separation. He couldn't bear the moments they were apart, and his world was askew. His thinking was clouded by a preoccupation with her. He was at the bottom, but he held on to all he had, his belief that he would someday be reunited with Rita and his son.

The empty days of the month passed, and he painfully earned his release. His payroll check arrived, and he at last got on the bus to join Rita and begin the home they both wanted for Joseph.

There would be hard times ahead for both of them, that was certain, but I couldn't deny the power of their love and the spirit they showed in finding a way to work things out.

CHAPTER 6

Darlene

My thoughts were still with Joe and Rita as I arrived at school this morning. I awakened my brain with a cup of hot coffee and relived with Michelle the events of the birth of Rita's baby.

Talking about successful outcomes made me feel encouraged. "S.A.M." must be weaving its magic, I thought, and we would keep on trying. I wanted S.A.M. to be a good experience for each girl who came to us. How difficult it was for me to find out that this was not always to be so.

Some of the girls who came to S.A.M. were married. The marriage always came after the pregnancy, and it usually was the couple's way of solving the problem of the baby, but often the hasty marriage created even more problems.

Such a couple were Darlene and Bob. They came together their first day at S.A.M. Darlene was talkative and seemed almost to overpower Bob, even though he was eight years older than she. Bob was quiet, and an odor of alcohol surrounded him. They sought out the couch and sat snuggled together as I tried to explain the procedure for enrolling, hoping that part of Darlene's attention was with me. Bob remained silent as he stroked Darlene's arm, twisting her wedding ring about on her finger. Darlene asked some questions about homework and school hours. We then walked through the school so that Darlene could meet the girls. Darlene draped herself on Bob's shoulder as they walked through the building. They seemed clinging and inseparable. Bob's amorous expression never changed.

Darlene was a tall, long-legged girl with dyed red hair. Her blue eyes were heavily outlined with black makeup that glistened on her eyelids. Her young skin was clean and clear except below the chin line where she had neglected to wash her neck.

Bits and pieces of her story came out as Darlene became more comfortable. She was a capable student but, when I went over the class record with her, I asked about the lack of credits in the tenth grade.

"Oh, that," she said, "well, I screwed around a lot then and never went to school. I guess it was the cocaine that really kept me from going to school. I was nervous all the time and couldn't concentrate on anything. When I did go, we used to get high in the bathroom—but I'm all over that now and want to go to school."

Darlene decided to enroll, and she and Bob left. Darlene said, "See ya tomorrow."

The next day I assigned classes for her to make up the lost credits and she started working with new pencils and notebook. Darlene was seventeen and Bob was twenty-five. She talked a lot about him in glowing terms.

One morning a few weeks later the girls came to tell me that Darlene was crying. I went to her, and the first thing she shrieked was, "I can't stand Bob! If I weren't so big and pregnant I'd go out on him just to make him mad. He is just a fuckin' alcoholic and I can't live with that! Every night he stays up late listening to the stereo—drinking—I can't get any sleep and I come to school so damned tired and nervous. I've had one nervous breakdown and I know the signs. I need more sleep. I tell him how I feel, but he just doesn't pay any attention. I think I'm going to flip out or something."

"Do you think it would help to have Bob come here after school and you and he could talk to Mrs. Hartley?"

"I don't need to talk to her, but I'll tell her what I want her to say to Bob. Yeah, if he's sober I'll give it a try—I'll call him and see."

Darlene said that Bob would come, and I called Grace to see if she was available. Grace had an appointment in the afternoon but she would try to reschedule it later in order to come.

When the school day ended, Darlene was gone. She had slipped out unnoticed with the others on their way to the bus. A few minutes later, Grace rushed in almost out of breath, saying, "I don't know how I did it, but I made it."

"Darlene's not here. I never saw her leave. I am so sorry that it happened this way—that you went to so much trouble in rearranging your schedule to get over here."

Grace looked disappointed too, but said philosophically, "Well, if Darlene didn't want to talk it wouldn't have worked anyway."

Darlene wasn't in school the next week, and our calls to her were unanswered. Perhaps I had moved too quickly—I didn't know. I couldn't find her, and Bob was no help; he didn't know where she was either. She was constantly on my mind.

The next time I saw Darlene, she looked terrible. There were dark circles under her eyes, and she looked shaky and sick.

"Are you all right?" I asked.

"Don't ask me, I just feel terrible. I couldn't stand things the way they were, so I got drunk for the whole week. I guess it was a week," she said with her head in hands, "I don't know."

Darlene concerned me so much. She didn't seem to have any consideration or thought for the fetus inside her. It was as if the baby didn't matter. The only good sign was the fact that she had got herself together to come back to school. I would make sure she got in to see her doctor regularly and then wait it out until she came to us. I would make myself available any time.

Little by little during our afternoon talks, she offered more and more of herself. She wanted both Grace Hartley and me to tell Bob the things that were wrong with him and what he was to do. She would say, "I can't get through to him. If you could just tell him what I want, things would get better between us."

We tried to make it clear to Darlene that we wouldn't be spokesmen for her, but she continued to try to manipulate us as well as the girls in S.A.M. Bob's side hadn't been heard yet, and it would be only fair to both of them if they would come together and talk things out.

Finally, they planned to come in after school. Grace and I realized that it probably wouldn't turn out, but we would be ready anyway.

A rusty, gray VW pulled into the parking space outside our window. Inside sat Darlene and Bob. They remained in the car for a while as they seemed to be arguing. Darlene got out and slammed the car door, leaving Bob with the choice of either taking off or following her. Four-letter words from their conversation floated through the open window.

"I hate that son of a bitch," Darlene said as she tore open the door. "He makes me so mad."

Bob walked in. His lips were tightly holding in the words he wanted to say. His face was an angry red. I looked at Grace, and she read my thoughts: What do I do now? I was relieved when she carried the conversation. At the moment things were beyond me.

Darlene and Bob sat down on the couch and glared at each other. Finally Darlene said, "Well, we made it—now what are we going to do?"

Grace answered, "I guess that's really up to you. We can sit here and waste everybody's time, or try to work things out if that's your choice. I've got lots of things I can be doing, but if you want to work together with this, I'd rather be right here."

"Come on, Bob, let's go," Darlene said, realizing that she was not going to be able to dominate the situation.

"Wait a minute, Darlene," Bob protested, "if we don't stay and at least try, then we aren't going to get any place." There was a long pause. Bob spoke again, "I never realized what marriage was all about. I just figured because we loved each other and the baby was on the way that we would be married. It just sort of seemed the right thing to do—but I'm working hard and Darlene's tired from going to school, and we just don't seem to be in love any more."

"What you really mean, Bob, is that you do everything for yourself and don't do anything for me at all—you stay up late with the stereo and TV on loud and I can't get any sleep. It's hard enough to sleep with this lump in my belly."

Grace broke in, "We aren't going to spend this time just arguing. From now on, if you are going to speak, do it without attacking one another."

"That's all she does is attack me, so to keep from hitting her I just get drunk to forget."

"Bob, I'm just telling you how I feel. I have to get things off my mind; I feel like I'll explode if I don't," Darlene yelled.

The conversation continued. Grace gave both Darlene and Bob a chance to see what each was doing in their relationship. If they could understand their behavior and their needs, and explain them to each other, then they could work on some changes—that is, if they were willing to make changes.

When the conversation ended, Darlene and Bob had their arms entwined. Grace had acted as facilitator, encouraging them both to talk honestly; this seemed to benefit them.

Before they left, Grace set up another time when they could come in to continue the conversation. It would take more than one conference for Darlene and Bob!

After Darlene and Bob left, I could not help but reflect on the early days of their marriage. They both had wanted to get married so badly. They had some opposition from her parents. Darlene's mother wasn't going to give her consent. I remember Darlene's describing how hard she was going to make it for her mother so that she would have to consent. She was going to make life around the house so miserable for her mother that she would have to agree to the marriage just to get Darlene out of the house. Darlene started on her plan, and her parents finally gave in. Darlene, the spoiled brat, got her way again. This same behavior was getting *in* her way now.

The on-again off-again romance continued. I was impatient for progress because soon the baby would add to the tense situation in the household. But progress was so slow.

Darlene's time was near, and I wanted her to be ready and prepared for her childbirth. Darlene had a fantasy that her labor and delivery would be different from the others, that she was going to breeze through it without discomfort. She refused to participate in our prepared childbirth classes because she felt that she didn't need them. Whatever her rationalizations, it was a different Darlene that called from the hospital after the birth of her daughter.

Her first words were, "Mrs. Whitfield, if I would have known that I was going to have twenty-six hours of labor, I would have listened more. It wasn't anything like I'd expected. It was just awful. I don't even want to think about it."

"How's your little girl?" I asked. "I'll bet she's beautiful."

"Oh, she's O.K.—she looks like a prune, and she's sort of red."

"What did you name her?"

"Bob picked out the name Shannon. I'm still not used to it, but it's an O.K. name. My butt hurts so bad I can hardly stand it. I have been just lying around this hospital. I can't wait to get out of here."

"What are you going to do when you get home?"

"Well, I know one thing, Bob's going to feed this kid in the middle of the night. I'm not going to get up. He can just listen to her cry if he doesn't."

"We are all anxious to see her. When you are feeling better, maybe you can bring Shannon in for a visit," I invited.

"Yeah, I'll do that," Darlene responded without interest.

After I hung up, a chill ran through my body as I thought of this little child and her future.

Three weeks later Darlene and Shannon returned to class. She placed the baby in its crib and sat down on the couch. She gave me a fighting look that said, "I dare you to talk to me." With that I turned away. I had time—Darlene would have to come to me. I would wait and see.

Days went by. Finally she came into the office and sat down. Now I felt we were getting someplace. She was ready to talk. She might be receptive. Darlene began. Her first expressions were confusing, as if she were trying to say everything in one sentence.

She told of her unhappy childhood. Her mother had bouts with alcoholism. Her father had left home. She still saw them both, but mostly to use them for what she wanted. The paradox was that this unfortunate girl didn't know what she wanted. She had learned early to manipulate people. She was unable and unwilling to listen to others who could help her make her life more pleasant. Life was a day-to-day attempt to gratify her wishes. She had no long-range goals. Her struggle for mental survival was a constant encounter, and her emotional strength fluctuated from mental anguish to false hope. So far, the baby kept her from doing some of the impulsive things she had done in the past. I kept hoping she would realize how important she was to her baby and to the man she had married. Instead, it was painfully obvious that Darlene wanted to mold her environment and others to suit herself. She continued to blame others for her problems. She denied her mistakes. She couldn't see herself in relationship to her problems. Self-gratification was her greatest need; yet she was never satisfied.

As I listened and thought about Darlene, I still hoped that everything would turn out in a positive way and that she would find herself and reach a higher level of living. I knew we would need much more contact and time.

Darlene's attendance at school was poor. Her excuses ranged from being too tired to being too upset. She resisted making personal change and continued blaming others for her unhappiness. One day she would be in a rage over a problem in her marriage, then the next it was as if it had never happened. There seemed to be no continuity from day to day or week to week. Close contact and communication was impossible. Darlene was a constant frustration to both Grace and me. Everything we tried to do to help was ignored. She had her own way of behaving and rejected any counseling.

I grieved for the baby and the environment in which she would be raised. I grieved for Bob in this marriage that was brought on by an untimely pregnancy, but most of all, I grieved for Darlene, who was the only one who could make things right but who could not see beyond her own selfish needs. It seemed like such a great loss.

CHAPTER 7

Sandi

O rdinary days pased one by one, punctuated occasionally by the arrival of a new girl or the de-
parture of one who had completed her time at
S.A.M.

Organizing the routine of the school was at first difficult,
but by now I had detailed each girl's class program on cards
and could at any moment evaluate a student's work and
progress. When a girl needed assistance, I could spend
extra time with her alone. Certain days of the week were
designated for particular activities. The daily program con-
sisted of work on academic subject matter. Special activities
were offered on certain days as follows: Tuesday: crafts,
sewing, fibercrafts, and art. Wednesday: health education,
infant and child care, and preparation for childbirth with
the nurse's guidance. Friday, Grace's day for group discussion and individual conferences.

The girls were from different schools, were at different
grade levels, and proceeded according to their levels of
ability.

I started slowly and carefully designed the curriculum,
and little by little each girl began to take the responsibility

given to her. Managing the school records and office work, in addition to teaching, was a task in itself. The students at S.A.M., by necessity, had good lessons in self-direction.

Even with my emphasis on self-direction, my days were filled with the "one-to-one" activities of conjugating verbs, figuring percent, sewing a zipper, balancing a checkbook, explaining footnotes, listening to a student read, finding a lost knitting stitch, discussing current events and so on. Each day was different and unusual in itself. A few classes were taught in groups but most of the curriculum was designed to take into account the revolving nature of the enrollment. The girls worked continually, earning credits toward their graduation from high school.

On this particular Monday morning the telephone rang, beginning the first of a stream of early-morning calls. Michelle answered and transferred the call to me.

"It's long distance! from across the country," she said, her expression showing curiosity.

The woman on the phone identified herself as the mother of a pregnant teenager and asked about the school, credits, etc., and the requirements for entrance. I explained that the girl needed to be of school age, pregnant, and have a desire to complete her high-school education. She also was required to live within our school district to be eligible for enrollment.

"My daughter meets your requirements and will be living with her sister in your area until this whole thing is over. Can she enroll?"

"Oh, yes, she can, and I will send you the necessary papers."

A note of concern crept into the mother's voice as she said, "You know, she will be living so far away from home."

I assured her that S.A.M. always took good care of their students, but in her daugher's case I would take extra special care. "And your daughter's name?" I requested.

"Sandi," said her mother, adding, "That's her nickname. Her real name is Sandra."

"Fine," I said, "we shall be watching anxiously for Sandi's arrival."

The mother said, "Thank you," and then hung up.

Wow! I wondered how she could have known about us and came up with no other conclusion than—impossible!

Michelle asked, "A new student?"

"Yes indeed, and from so far away," I answered. We tried to imagine what Sandi might look like and what her story might be. We both concluded that she certainly would be lost for a while coming so far away from friends and family.

Weeks later, the door opened and a cute blonde rushed in.

"Hi, I'm Sandi," she announced. "I guess this must be the place. My mom called you a few weeks ago, remember?"

"Yes, I surely do. We have been waiting for you."

"Well, I wondered what a school for pregnant teenagers was like—this isn't bad. I think I'll like it here," she said with an impish grin.

Sandi acted as if she were on her first trip to Europe and was enjoying the tour already. She was high-spirited and excited about making the most of her trip. But, best of all, she certainly wasn't lost.

"While I'm here I want to go to the beach and get a good tan. I've heard lots about California and now I'm here. Yep, when I go back home I must have a good tan," Sandi bubbled. What a free and easy, happy spirit. Sandi won new friends quickly, and it wasn't long before she became the clown of the school. Just when she would be giving the punch line to a story, the girls would tease her about her accent. She would pretend to be hurt and insulted and, when she had convinced us, she would laugh and say, "You didn't believe me, did you?!" She was always good for a laugh, and she loved it.

One Friday, Grace's day, Sandi began the group by telling about her boyfriend. They were high-school sweethearts and the most admired couple of their school. He was going to study medicine after graduation. She was a cheerleader and also had plans for college. They were high-school seniors and involved in the whirl of activities of their last year.

Sandi described what happened when she told Mike that she was pregnant. He was delighted and proposed marriage, but before she could respond he whisked her to his house to tell his parents the good news about the coming marriage and the baby. His parents were equally excited and proposed a toast to the happy couple. Sandi couldn't get a word in edgewise. She kept thinking. "I don't want to get married. Everyone just assumes that we would be married, and now they haven't even given me a chance to say anything—how can I get out of this awful mess?"

From Mike's house they went to Sandi's. Her mother and little sister were there. Mike made the joyful announcement and Sandi's mom was stunned. She seemed to get herself together enough to offer feeble congratulations while "little sister" pumped Mike's hand up and down with juvenile exuberance. But Sandi still faked her happiness and worried about what her father would say when he got home. Mike suggested that he wait for his "father-in-law" to arrive, but Sandi asked that he leave so that they could all prepare for the father's arrival.

Her mother hugged her and said, "Oh, my little child —you're going to be married. Oh, we must make wedding plans. How do you feel? All of this is so sudden."

Sandi still couldn't express herself. Everything was snowballing into something bigger than she had ever expected. It was only that afternoon that she had told Mike and now, early evening, everything seemed so positive and final.

The heavy steps at the front door signaled Sandi that her father was about to enter. Now what! The whole complicated mess was going to get even more complicated. He was going to be mad and probably go after Mike with his shotgun, and Sandi would be locked in her room forever! (How the girls chuckled at this statement of Sandi's.) Sandi continued her story. "Oh what torture could be worse than this day," was her thought as the door opened. Her mother was in tears huddled in the corner, her sister was making wisecracks from the kitchen, and now her father entered the room.

"Hi, Dad," Sandi said with a fake smile.

"What's going on here?" he said.

A tearful, "Sandi's going to be married and have a baby, too," came from the corner.

Crash, boom! The explosion came with her father's immediate reaction. "What the hell did you do a thing like that for? No daughter of mine is going to have to have a shotgun marriage. Where is that bastard? I'll kill him."

"I told you so, I told you so," came from the kitchen.

Hardly realizing what he had said, he turned to see the tears now on his daughter's cheeks. "Oh, sweetheart, how could this happen to us?"

The sound of ice cubes colliding in glasses depressed Sandi too. Now they were going to have a "drink" and there would be no time to settle anything.

Sandi didn't have dinner but went straight to bed. She tossed and turned all night thinking what she would do. She was the only one in the whole world who knew that she didn't want to get married. How could she untangle this complicated mess now that everyone had become involved?

Morning came so slowly. Sandi still hid in her room. Finally, after she thought everyone had left, she crept to the kitchen, only to find that her father was still at the breakfast table. She was surprised to see that he hadn't gone to work. Now, what else would happen? But his ire was spent and he began to talk to her as he had when she was a little girl.

"Sweetie, tell me how you feel."

"Oh, Dad, I'm so upset and confused. I thought I loved Mike, and now the thought of marriage scares me. He just assumed that we would get married, and his family seemed so happy that they would be grandparents—I wanted to say no, no, no! but somehow I just couldn't. Why? Why did this all have to happen to me?"

"Whatever happens, your mom and I will be behind you. I'm sorry I got so mad last night. I guess I just reacted without thinking. Now we should be thinking about what to do. You know, I bet your sister Cindy would love to have you stay with her in California."

"Daddy, that's a terrific idea. I just knew that you would come up with something great. That's what I want to do. I'll go to California and stay with her!"

"Your mom and I will find out all the details—you don't need to worry any more."

"You knew, didn't you, Dad, that all the time I didn't want to get married and couldn't keep this baby. How did you know all that? I guess because you are the greatest dad ever!"

"You see," she turned to the group listening attentively, "that is how I got to California. Wow, I am so glad to be here!" One of the girls sitting quietly in the group asked what happened to Mike and his family. Sandi explained that they met with her family one night and talked everything out. Mike and his parents were crushed and disappointed, but Sandi was firm. Her decision was final. Soon after that she was on her way across the country.

There were no other comments. The hour was up and the group broke for lunch. One by one, they decided to sit outside on the grass and enjoy the warm California sun.

Grace and I were so involved in conversation that, before we realized it, we were the only ones eating inside. We finished lunch and decided to join the girls. We opened the back door and were struck by the sight before us. There was our pregnant class all dressed in bikini bathing suits exposing their bare stomachs to the sun's rays. I shrieked with surprise, and Sandi said, "I told everyone to wear bathing suits under their clothes today just for fun. I hope you don't mind."

"Me mind? What about the neighbors and the cars going by on the street and the people working in the offices?"

We sat down in the "pumpkin patch"—Grace and I looked at one another. We appeared so out of place with dresses, stockings and heels, trying to get comfortable on the grass. Grace kept looking out of the corner of her eye to see if anyone was coming. What if the boss arrived, or even worse, the superintendent. Maybe it was just my imagination, but it seemed as if the small airplanes usually flying with direction and some purpose were coming in closer for a look. What a congregation!

The girls realized how out of place they looked, and that the open backyard of the school wasn't like home. Sandi said, "I don't care if anyone sees me like this. They will just know that I'm going to have a baby—that's O.K."

"That's O.K. for you but not for the whole school," another girl said. "I think we should sunbathe at home if we want to, but not at school."

"O.K., you guys—it was a good trick on Mrs. Hartley and Mrs Whitfield anyway," Sandi said with a wink.

The bus didn't come too soon. I realized that my girls were just like any other high-school girls, but they still found it hard to visualize their pregnancies. They were so very young.

It seemed as if funny circumstances followed Sandi around. Some were carefully contrived by her, but others were not.

One morning a call came in saying that the water would be shut off for a few hours. They were repairing the street outside.

Sandi decided that we would just walk down to the corner gas station if anyone needed to use the restroom. Well, with the lack of modern conveniences and the power of suggestion, it wasn't long before the whole school needed to visit the gas station. With all the necessary permissions of a field trip, we took off for the corner. Sandi led the group, using her cheerleading expertise to add a certain flair to the march. When we arrived, the people at the station gawked at the procession. The line at the "Ladies" stretched around to the front of the gas pumps. A woman got out of her car and stood patiently at the end of the line. She looked puzzled at the unusual line before her. Sandi, seeing the woman's strange look, seized the opportunity and said, "You know how it is when you're pregnant!" Giggles rippled down the line.

The gas-station episode was good for much laughter for weeks, and as those weeks passed the time for the birth of Sandi's baby came near.

She was always sure that her baby would be placed for adoption. The only thing that complicated her life was the

fact that Mike had decided to come out for a visit and to be
here when the baby was born. She decided that, if that was
what he wanted to do, it was O.K. with her. But their
relationship had ended, and they saw no hope of getting
back together again. However, if he wanted to visit, he
certainly had the right to.

It was 10:30 A.M. I remember the time so vividly because it was at that time that Sandi asked for the watch with
the large second hand. We used the "watch" only for timing labor contractions and typing tests. Since Sandi wasn't
taking typing, it was reasonable to assume that she was in
labor. Michelle flipped her steno pad over to a clean page
and began noting the time and duration of each contraction. Sandi laughingly said she was just fooling, but I felt
the hardness of her stomach with my hand. "Oh, it's probably just false labor—nothing to get excited about," she
said. Well, we would just have to wait and see.

There was an air of joviality, because no one could really
tell if Sandi was teasing again and the class guarded itself
against being fooled. She would nod to Michelle who
would note the time.

The contractions were ten minutes apart and had already
lasted for two hours. I asked Michelle for Sandi's folder
with the doctor's name and number, but she could only
reply, "Don't bug me—I'm just trying to maintain." Michelle was calm on the surface but barely holding on
inside.

Sandi called her doctor, and he suggested that she come
to the hospital when the contractions were regular and
about 5 minutes apart. She still had plenty of time. Then
Sandi confided to me that her sister was out of town and
asked if I would stay with her during labor. For the first
time, she looked very alone. Her young face beamed when
I said I would be delighted to be with her. I suggested she

come home with me after school and I would take her to the hospital and stay with her the entire time. Sandi appeared calm and relaxed.

I had never volunteered to be with any of the girls in labor because I felt it was the place for a father or family, but Sandi had no one and I couldn't let her go through childbirth alone.

My thoughts found me anticipating the long hours ahead. I hoped that everything would be normal and that I would have the strength to be the support that Sandi needed.

Michelle's steno pad had a long list of times written on it. First A.M. and now P.M. Everyone was in good spirits. Sandi wanted to play one last trick on the bus driver before we left. We watched for the big yellow bus and planned how she would tell the bus driver she was in labor and give instructions on how to get to the nearby hospital. The driver was always afraid that one of the girls would begin labor on the bus, and she had even taken a course on emergency childbirth but never wanted to put it into practice. She would say, kiddingly, "I don't want any of you to begin labor on this school bus."

Sandi saw it as a golden opportunity for a practical joke and rehearsed the words she would say several times.

"Here comes the bus!" Michelle shouted. We trooped out to the curb. I went along to add a certain air of authenticity to the story, and I *had* to see the look on the driver's face.

Sandi walked up confidently to the open door of the bus with her well-prepared speech. "I just thought I'd tell you that I'm in labor and today, instead of taking me home, you can go directly to the hospital!"

The bus driver screamed and reeled back in her seat.

Her glasses flew back on her head, and if she hadn't been wearing a seat belt she probably would have gone out the window. The girls burst out laughing and assured her that Sandi wouldn't be riding today. She breathed a sigh of relief and began laughing, too. "I just knew it—I knew someone would be in labor."

Sandi was delighted at the effectiveness of her joke and walked with me to my car. A girl paused to say, "Mrs. Whitfield, you always get so excited about everyone's labor like it was the first." I surely did, because even though I had been through it many times it was always the first for each girl.

We drove home and on the way picked up my daughter from school. I tried to make Sandi as comfortable as possible while I made arrangements for my family. I was really in luck. Our son was invited to a friend's house and our daughter stayed with a neighbor. What a relief to have everything work out so smoothly. I called Sandi's mother to say that everything was progressing smoothly, and she and Sandi talked, both trying to make each other feel at ease.

The time seemed to go so slowly as she sat there on the couch. My little dog sat beside her with an ear on her large stomach, sensing, I am sure, that a baby was to be born.

We both decided together that it was time to leave for the hospital. As I drove through the rush-hour traffic I wanted to honk the horn and say, "Let us through, a baby will be born tonight."

At the hospital she was whisked away in a wheelchair to the delivery floor. I found my way to the "Father's Waiting Room" and sat down with a group of nervous fathers watching the evening news. They looked anxiously at me and I at them. "We are about to be fathers, but what are you?"

"I'm about to be...I don't know...an interested by-stander?" Inside I knew I was Sandi's strength if she need-ed me.

A nurse came to say I could come into Sandi's room. At first we laughed about the surroundings and the circum-stances, but soon Sandi's labor became more intense. She put into practice her prepared childbirth techniques. I smoothed her blonde hair, and she said, "I'm so glad you're here, Mrs. Whitfield, I didn't want to be alone—don't ever leave me." The doctor came in and asked me to wait out-side while he checked her progress. She didn't want me to leave, but he convinced her that I would just be outside the door and would come right back.

When the doctor came out he confided that the baby was larger than anticipated and that he hoped a Caesarean section wouldn't be needed.

It was midnight now, and Sandi was very, very tired. She cried and wondered how much longer she could hold on. I held her hand and talked about many things, trying to keep her spirits up, but I could see she was slipping and losing control.

Suddenly her eyes rolled back in her head and her whole body began to shake convulsively. As she thrashed about on the bed, I grabbed the "call" button and screamed, "Nurse, Nurse!" The convulsions were more violent, and I yelled even louder. The nurse took one look at Sandi and ran down the hall for the doctor. He shouted orders as he adjusted the oxygen mask on Sandi's blue face. Shots were administered through the I.V., and there was a flurry of nurses around her bedside. It seemed like an eter-nity before the convulsions ceased. I stood with my back against the wall, using it to hold me up—my knees were so wobbly. Oh, Sandi, you have been through so much.

Please don't let anything else happen. Nothing else could happen. Please don't die.

The nurses and doctor worked together like a well-practiced team, and the shaking stopped. The room, just a moment before noisy with violence, suddenly was still. I heard Sandi's soft voice say, "Mrs. Whitfield, where are you?"

"I'm here—right here beside you, Sandi," I said, my voice cracking. I patted her with compassion.

"What are all these people doing here?"

"Oh, they were just here to help you. It won't be long now."

The doctor called an associate, and plans were made to proceed with the Caesarean section. The nurse began to move the bed, and Sandi began to cry, "Don't leave me. Don't leave me." I walked down the hall holding her hand as they rolled the hospital bed to the delivery room. The nurse nodded and whispered to me that I had to wait outside. The doors to the delivery room closed, but I heard Sandi's pleading cry, "Please don't leave me, Mrs. Whitfield, please, please, please don't leave me."

Her words echoed in my head as I walked helplessly down the corridor to the waiting room. It was excruciating torture. When I arrived at the fathers' waiting room I felt my hot face wet with tears. I sank down into a soft chair while the late, late show on TV droned on and on.

I suddenly remembered that Sandi wanted me to call Mike. My last coin tinkled into the pay phone. It rang and rang. Then a sleepy voice said, "Hello?"

"Mike, Sandi is in the delivery room now."

"I'll be right there. I'm coming right away." The dial tone buzzed in my ear.

There was a new batch of fathers in the waiting room,

and we went though the same exchange of glances about my being there. Sandi would have appreciated the humor in the situation. But I was spent and waited silently for Mike.

The elevator door opened and a young man jumped out looking left and right.

"Mike, is that you? Come in here. Sandi is still in the delivery room." I explained what had happened and he sat leaning forward, resting his elbows on his knees, holding his head in his hands in silence.

The double doors from the delivery suite opened, and a nurse rolled a baby in a warming incubator to the nursery.

"Is that my baby?" Mike asked. I was sure it was, because at this hospital only the adopted babies came out without their mothers.

The time dragged on, and Mike and I sat absorbed in our thoughts. Our worried looks cued concern from the fathers waiting there.

The double doors opened again, and this time it was Sandi. Shock showed all over Mike's face as he saw the network of plastic tubes emanating from her tired body. Sandi managed a slight smile and said, "We had a boy, 9 lb. 3 oz." The three of us went together to the maternity section.

"Thank you so much, Mrs. Whitfield," Sandi said, "I couldn't have made it alone." With that, Sandi was soon asleep, and Mike and I went to the nursery. We stood outside on the balcony looking into the window. The fog swirled around us as the sky lightened in the east. Mike began to sob uncontrollably as he saw his baby closely for the first time.

"I was big like him when I was born," he cried. "He looks just like my baby pictures." He leaned on me for support, and the two of us, eyes blurred with tears, looked into the nursery at the newborn child, thinking about the past and wondering about the future of this new life before us.

CHAPTER 8

Alexandria

The buzzing of the alarm clock brought me to my senses. I had been in bed just two short hours and my whole body was numb with fatigue, but it was a new day and school awaited me.

The experience of only a few hours before clung to me like a shroud. I got up and went about the usual morning tasks, but my thoughts were still at the hospital with Sandi.

I hardly remembered driving to school. The drama of Sandi's childbirth was as real to me as if it were happening all over again.

I would call Sandi's mother after the doctor's early-morning check and give her the details of her daughter's condition.

As I opened the door at school, Michelle smiled a "good morning." I sat down heavily in my chair. It was obvious that I was still in shock.

"What did Sandi have?" she asked.

"A boy."

"You look terrible. What's wrong?" Michelle questioned. I explained in detail my experience of the night before. Michelle was stunned. We sat in the office in silence. We didn't even hear the school bus pull up to the curb, and when the door opened with laughing girls we were startled. My mind wasn't at school this day. I hoped that I could make it through without giving myself away. As the teacher, I seemed to be the strength, the model, sometimes the mother for my girls, but I wasn't super-human. I was just like any other person, with areas of sensitivity and weakness. I didn't want to tell the whole story again just then. I wanted to find the right time and place so that the ones who hadn't delivered wouldn't be alarmed. They were emotional enough, and I didn't want to add to their worries.

The first thing the girls wanted to do was call Sandi and wish her well. They always rallied around the one who had just given birth, to give her support and add to their own confidence when it became their turn. Even though our preparation for childbirth was extensive, it was very help-ful to hear a first-hand account directly from the hospital. I held off the call until afternoon, giving Sandi more time to recover.

The day dragged on. Calls were answered, records were checked, classes were taught. When I called Sandi's moth-er, I told her everything that I thought a mother would want to know. She wasn't alarmed, just thankful that the ordeal was over and things could get back to normal.

Sandi was delighted about the call from school and seemed to be in good spirits. She told us how she teased the doctor and nurses and was causing a mild riot at the hos-pital just to get her money's worth. She was back to her old self again. Even the incision on her abdomen reminded her of a little smile and it would be (just barely) hidden below the edge of her bikini. Her suntanned tummy reminded her of a deflated balloon, and everyone got a good laugh from that.

When finally school was over I breathed a sigh of relief. It was like finishing a race in last place but nonetheless finishing. I was so tired and discouraged. Who was I to be the one who influenced or tried to intercede in the lives of these girls! It was an awesome responsibility and I wasn't sure that I was the right person for the job. I would have given anything to have prevented what Sandi went through but seemed powerless. I felt like giving up and letting someone else take this job and all the trauma that went with it.

While I was lost in my thoughts I hadn't noticed before that the little yellow sports car was still parked outside. Its presence meant that Alexandria was still here, and I left my desk to find her.

Alexandria was sitting at the couch fumbling with a knitting project that she was trying to finish for a grade. The needles would stop and start as she tried to make headway. Finally, she threw the project on the floor. "I just can't do anything right. Look at this mess. I'm a big disappointment to everybody."

Alexandria was from a wealthy, well-known family in town. She always had plenty of money to spend, which she did often, persuading a friend to buy alcohol that she shared with her group of friends. Her parents didn't approve of her boyfriend or her "gang" and last year sent her to Europe to try to change her way of life. She loved Europe and European men. When I asked her what she liked best about the trip, she said, "Sex European style." She was fast-living, and now her pregnancy cramped her style. She was on probation, which also put limits on her; she had been caught shoplifting in a grocery store. She had the money in her purse but, for the excitement, tried to sneak things out. When the manager approached her in the parking lot, Alexandria offered to pay for the items and tried to talk her way out of it; she was a good manipulator. The manager called the police instead. Since it wasn't her first offense, she landed in Juvenile Hall. During her stay there she became friends with Joe. Joe was a loser from the start. His rap sheet read like the Sunday *Times*, but Alexandria felt that he needed her, and she would baby him and buy the drugs he seemed unable to do without.

At the present time the rift between Alexandria and her parents seemed irreparable, but it hadn't always been that way. During a quiet moment she related to me the events of the day when she told her parents about her pregnancy. It seemed like one shock after another when it came to Alexandria's actions. After the initial explosion was over, however, things settled down to the extent that Alexandria and her parents were speaking again. That night when she was in bed her father entered her bedroom. Thinking she was asleep, he bent down over her and smoothed her hair. He carefully tucked the covers in around her as he had done when she was a little girl and quietly said, "I love you." Alexandria pretended to be asleep, and as he left the room she wanted to say, "I don't deserve you. I'm just a big disappointment and always have been." But she remained silent.

Living at home was unbearable for Alexandria. Her mother had certain rules and regulations that she expected to be obeyed, and Alexandria was rebellious. "Nice girls don't stay out so late," and, "If you are going to be a lady you don't associate with people who aren't of the same background," were examples of her mother's standards. Alexandria felt she could never live up to these standards, and since she couldn't, she would just go on from day to day waiting for the opportunity to leave home.

That day came very soon. She gathered her things, left a note, and moved to a cheap downtown apartment with Joe.

Then they applied for and received welfare. Her parents disowned her in order to keep their place in society.

In the three-room apartment their romance flourished. It was Alexandria who asked questions about positions and techniques during intercourse. She wanted permission to take days off from school so that she and Joe could spend the whole day together in bed! But the love nest wasn't as happy as they had planned. The realities and the expenses of living together were unforeseen. Alexandria was used to having plenty of money, and now even the thought of a budget was foreign to her. As time passed there were more and more arguments about bills and payments.

They both continued to use drugs and alcohol, and the expense put a crimp in the food budget. She wasn't eating or sleeping properly, and it was at this point that she stayed after school to cry on my shoulder.

"Help me, Mrs. Whitfield, I just can't go on. Things just haven't worked out. I don't know what's happening. I thought that things were bad at home with my parents, but with Joe it's the same old fighting. I can't stand it anymore."

I was so tired that I could hardly think straight. I had to come up with something so that Alexandria could make it through the rest of the day and night. Maybe Grace could come over, and the three of us could work something out for now, or at least comfort Alexandria so that she could go on a little longer. Alexandria had always liked Grace, so I knew that she would be happy to see her if she could come.

Grace always knew that when I called for help it was important, and she would do everything to wind things up at her office so that she could come over right away. She would say philosophically, "If your girls need help, this is where I am today." As the telephone rang, I hoped she wouldn't be away at one of her other schools. The voice at the end of the line gave me hope that she could come, and indeed she did.

Her face at the door gave me a feeling of relief. The three of us began talking. Grace, even unaware of the full impact of my night before, carried me through the afternoon and comforted Alexandria so that she seemed much relieved. There would be more counseling for Alexandria with Grace, but for now, as the little yellow sports car sped off, we felt some confidence that the things that could be resolved now had been touched upon and Alexandria would be in school tomorrow.

Grace's eyes on me during the talk carried a thousand questions, and after Alexandria left she waited for me to speak. I retold and relived last night. "Sometimes I feel so alone, and I don't really know if I'm doing enough or even the right thing. Sometimes this school and the girls are too much for me."

"Cathy, you're tired now—worn out. It's easy to lose sight of all the wonderful things you do at a time like this."

Grace always had a comforting, warm way with people, and now it was my turn. I had a chance to unload all my frustrations. It was very rare to talk with anyone who really knew the kinds of things that I went through and the intense trauma of the days at S.A.M. No one could really understand unless they were involved directly. I never talked much to others about the details of my girls, because I usually was given a slanted response depending upon the person's bias; and at the end of the day I didn't feel like working through prejudices on top of the problems relating to teenage pregnancies. It was so good to be able to free myself from the burden upon my shoulders. Grace listened and listened and then gave me a picture of my true worth and value to the program, and I slowly began to feel better.

It was dark as I finally locked S.A.M.'s door. I would surely get a much-needed rest tonight.

Alexandria attended regularly each day, and I am sure part of her reason was to get away from Joe. She seemed to have nowhere else to go. I tried to think of places for her to stay, but she disliked moving and disliked staying. I hoped she could work through some of the problems before her baby arrived, which would be in about two months. She was still debating what to do about the baby. She couldn't picture actually how it would be, staying home and caring for a child, but she wanted the baby because it was something to have and love, and this she needed so desperately. Also, keeping a baby was a good way to get back at her parents, especially her mother, because she then was a mother herself and it would be a visible source of embarrassment to her strict Victorian mother.

Unfortunately, I had no contact with the mother. She wouldn't return my calls and never accepted my invitations to come to school. I really felt stumped. It was quite a lesson when I finally learned that I couldn't help someone who didn't want help.

So there I was in the middle of a situation that involved a girl who seemed to be keeping her baby to spite her mother, a rigid mother who refused help, a boyfriend interested only in sex and drugs, and a bewildered father who had love to give but was always put in his place by his wife.

Then, suddenly, I got an idea. I would try to make contact with Alexandria's father while he was at work. It was my only hope. Perhaps he would be receptive—I had to try.

I grabbed the telephone and dialed the work number that Alexandria had put on her admittance card. The telephone rang and rang. Finally, a female voice answered, "Canadey Corporation."

"This is Mrs. Whitfield, Alexandria's teacher. May I speak with Mr. Canadey?"

The next thing I heard was, "Mr. Canadey's office." I explained who I was again and was put on hold. Finally the secretary came on the line to tell me that Mr. Canadey would return my call. I felt as though I had failed and wouldn't be hearing from him again.

That afternoon, a voice on the telephone said, "This is Mr. Canadey returning your call." I was surprised and relieved to hear his voice.

"I wanted to talk with you because I'm concerned about Alexandria and need your help. Her living situation just isn't working out, and I wondered if you could give me any suggestions."

In a deep voice, he said, "I'll give it some thought. You know that Alexandria's mother won't let her come back home."

"Do you have any friends or relatives who might take her in on a temporary basis?" I asked. "She needs someone to care for her right now."

"Well, I suppose I could ask my sister, Alexandria's aunt. She has a spare bedroom and always liked Alexandria as a child. I'll ask her and then call you back in a day or so."

"Thank you, Mr. Canadey; this could make a big difference for her."

At first Alexandria was apprehensive about moving in with her aunt, but she agreed that it was better than her present situation. After the initial adjustment period was over, I could see a change in Alexandria. She was more relaxed and I felt, at least for the present, it was a good place for her. The aunt visited school and I was encouraged by her interest.

Grace and I spent many afternoons together in counseling with Alexandria. We hoped she would gain in confidence and self-esteem.

One afternoon Alex blurted out,

"Sometimes I just have to get away as far as possible from my parents. Other times I just feel defeated."

"Don't lose heart, Alex," we encouraged, "you really have all that you need inside you to succeed."

Improvement was slow, and the time was approaching for the birth of the baby. I still felt uneasy about the whole situation. Alexandria was positive about keeping the baby. She was going to provide the best she could for her baby with her aunt's help. I was grateful for Alexandria that her aunt had been willing to step in and be the mother she needed.

One Monday morning we received a call from Alexandria. She was in the hospital. She had given birth to a 5 lb. 8 oz. baby and had a normal delivery and, as she described it, a beautiful little girl. I was relieved to hear that, at least for now, everything was happy and "normal."

A week and a half later Alexandria's aunt brought her to school to show off her new baby. She seemed nervous as she clumsily carried infant seat, baby, and diaper bag through the door.

She sat on the couch with the girls around her, describing her labor and delivery. As she talked, she moved the baby uncertainly from lap to shoulder and back to her lap again with shaking hands. I restrained myself from asking to hold the little one because I could see how desperately Alex wanted to do everything herself.

It was good that Alexandria and her baby would be returning to S.A.M. until she was physically and emotionally ready for regular school. I would still have some months to counsel with her, but I was afraid it would take a longer time than we might have for Alex to understand the reasons for her behavior in the past and make the changes that would help her to get along successfully, and eventually be able to heal the scars of the severed relationship with her family.

CHAPTER 9

Elyse

"**H**ow strange and lonely it is sitting here on this airplane getting farther and farther away from home each minute.

"I won't be starting back to school this September with all my friends. It's so hard to believe this whole thing! I'm still me, fifteen and a half, straight 'A' student, school paper editor, class chairman, and lucky (I thought) to have Robby, my steady guy.

"Gee, the hours Robby and I used to talk about everything, and the neat times we had at school with our friends and on dates. It seemed so right and so natural for us to love each other! We must have been pretty innocent, because it all turned out to be not just a mistake we made, but a really horrible nightmare.

"Boy, when I told Mom, and she told Dad that I was pregnant, instead of them trying to understand or help me, all they could think of was how to get rid of me!

"It's not like I wasn't already worried enough when I thought I might be pregnant! When I told Robby, he said, 'Don't worry about it. We'll work it all out.'

"Wow, how can a person change so much? He must have

been very scared. Next thing I knew, his parents were over at my house talking to my parents, and they gave my parents money for my trip out to stay with Grandpa and Grandma! Oh, Robby, can't you see how awful this is? We can't ever be friends again. It's all blown apart. Does anybody know how I feel? Does anybody care any more?

"Oh, great! Tears and crying again. That's all I do. Well, who wouldn't? Mom sure let me know how disappointed she was in me. Sure I feel like a 'bad girl,' a tramp. It's so rotten. I've let everyone down.

"Gee! what high mountains down there. If the plane crashed here no one would ever find us.

"Two more hours 'til I get there. My stomach hurts. I'll have to stay with Grandpa and Grandma for seven months. What a drag for all of us!"

Even in regular classes, a teacher may wait many years or never have a student so amazingly superior in all aspects of human functioning as I was privileged to have when Elyse arrived at S.A.M.

Elyse's home was in Indiana. She was one of five children. Her dad was a manufacturing company executive, and her mom was a lab technician at the local hospital.

In high school Elyse was active in student body affairs. Her natural interest in the world about her made it impossible for her to stay uninvolved. Her fine intellectual capacity caused her to perceive beyond the scope of most of her peers and of many adults; yet she was, first of all, a fifteen-year-old girl caught up in all the feelings, pressures, problems, and enthusiasms of her age.

When Elyse told her parents she was pregnant, her mother was shocked and immediately let Elyse know she was suddenly a bad girl—no longer a fine student, a joy to the family, etc. Arrangements were made quickly by her mother to send Elyse to California to stay with relatives until the baby was born.

Elyse found herself flying out to her grandparents before she had time to think.

It was a homesick, lonely girl who came into my office that first day of the fall semester. Her grandfather left her after introducing himself and Elyse. What a kind, gentle man he seemed to be.

I looked at Elyse sitting forlornly in the chair at my desk. Her big blue eyes searched the faces and the room for some sign of comfort or familiarity.

"Tell me, Elyse, about your high school back home," I began.

I could see this subject was too painful for now, so I asked about her due date for the baby and then told her a little about S.A.M., reassuring her that it might seem a little awkward at first, but that I felt sure she would be more comfortable in a few days. Elyse was pale and said she didn't feel well. When I suggested she lie down, she agreed quickly. I showed her our little room with the bed in it.

About a half hour later I went to check on Elyse and saw she had been crying. I put my hand on her shoulder, saying, "You just don't feel good at all today, do you Elyse?" She shook her head, saying nothing, but tears again began to stream down her face.

"What can I do that will help today, Elyse?"

"I don't know. I just feel so homesick for my friends and my family. And I don't feel good either. I feel like I'm always going to throw up."

"You can call your doctor from here, and he may have something you can take that will help you with nausea." Elyse seemed a little surprised at the thought of her taking that independent action, but the idea appealed to her and she decided to make the call.

Elyse followed me into the office, where I got the telephone directory out for her and then left her alone.

A few minutes later Elyse came out of the office looking pleased.

"How did it go?" I asked.

"I am going in to pick up a prescription after school today."

"Good for you, Elyse," I smiled. "It's crafts period, and you can see the different projects the girls are working on and think about what you want to make."

Once Elyse was settled down at the table I left the room, as I knew it was important for the other girls to talk to Elyse and get acquainted.

I busied myself in the office. A series of telephone calls kept me tied up longer than I realized. When I looked up after completing a call, Jinny was standing there with Elyse beside her.

"Mrs. Whitfield, can I show 'Lyse that new book you just got with all those neat big color pictures?"

"You sure can, Jinny," I said as I got the book from the cupboard. "Ah," I thought as I watched Jinny and Elyse leave the office together, "the magic of S.A.M. is beginning to work."

The days began to fall into a pattern at school. And the weeks went by.

We arranged to have a tutor come early each day to work with Elyse on geometry. She was always there on time and eager to learn. She worked diligently on all the courses she was taking at S.A.M. She was a fine student and interested in academic learning.

Elyse talked to the girls and took part in all of S.A.M.'s activities, but she was set apart by her keen mind. She was always way ahead of everyone else in her thinking and her ability to see and project her thinking into far-reaching areas.

Elyse had been working out ways to provide the best possible life for her baby through adoption. She talked at length with her doctor, who put her in touch with an attorney. After long conversations, it was agreed that Elyse could interview the couples interested in adopting her baby.

Details were attended to carefully by Elyse. She did not brush off any responsibility she felt was hers to assume. At fifteen years, she had the maturity that is often hard-won for a forty-year-old.

I knew it was a great burden on Elyse to have to deal with all those very emotional decisions. The pressure was not good for her, and there seemed to be little relief for her in anything else. She was bored living in an apartment complex that was designed for wealthy elderly people. Elyse sometimes exercised in the gym room there or went swimming.

She felt obligated to be cheerful with her grandparents because they were so good to her, but she was bored and depressed much of the time.

The journal I had asked Elyse to keep revealed these and many others feelings.

> "Season of pain
>   Fallen from grace—endlessly.
>   Why do I cry? It can't be helped;
>   Love is such a tenuous thing."

The days dragged on for Elyse. Yet in group she would say she still had many things to do in connection with the adoption arrangements for the baby.

She wrote a letter to the adopting parents to be kept in a safe deposit box until the child was old enough to want to read it. In the letter she told the child why she could not be a good parent at fifteen years of age, that she wanted to provide him the best possible life and had decided that giving him good parents was the best way to do it.

She said she told her child many other things that were just between the two of them.

Knowing the depth of Elyse's feelings, I was sure this child would feel wealthy and really cared for someday when he read the letter.

There is always the possibility with "my" young mothers that a Caesarean section will be necessary. When Elyse was told this by her doctor, she was unhappy, realizing that her return home might be further delayed by a longer recovery period. However, she accepted the fact that it might be necessary.

The due date arrived. Then five more days passed. Elyse faithfully finished up every detail of schoolwork and found herself just waiting.

She slept late one morning for some reason, and when she awakened she felt a contraction. She began timing and found the contractions were already two minutes apart. Surprised, she telephoned the doctor, who told her she was farther into labor than Elyse thought possible.

Elyse had slept through the early hours of labor and was now to go straight to the hospital. She was nervous when she called to tell me about it.

"It started in the night while I was sleeping, Mrs. Whitfield. I kept tossing and turning, thinking it was false labor again. I remember I had weird dreams, but I never thought I was in labor. My grandparents let me sleep late.

They said they heard me in the night tossing and moaning. When I awoke, I was scared because I thought labor was just starting and I couldn't stand it like this. If this was beginning labor, I'd never make it to the end. I got panicky. As soon as I get to the hospital, I know I'll feel better."

"Good luck. I know you'll do just fine, you're so well prepared. I'll be thinking of you, and call us and let us know how it was for you."

Just before school was over, Elyse called to tell us she had delivered a beautiful baby girl with fair skin and blonde hair. "Just like her Mommy!" I exclaimed to Elyse.

"Yes, but she looks like Robby, too," Elyse added, wistfully.

"She is so beautiful, Mrs. Whitfield. I've fallen in love with her even though it can only be a temporary love affair! When I hold her, I can talk to her, and it's almost as if she understands why I'm giving her up," Elyse exclaimed happily.

I visited Elyse the following afternoon. She talked of her visits with the baby and how when she held her she stopped crying. She was so wound up—intense in her excitement. I could see why the doctor had prescribed tranquilizers. Her blood pressure had soared, too, and she was on other medication.

Elyse told me how wonderful the future parents had been, calling her to see how she felt and telling her they had seen the baby and how very lovely she was. "It really made me sure I'd chosen the best parents." The girls asked why she spent so much time with the baby at the hospital. Elyse answered, "How could I have really known my gift without being with her?"

Elyse called me the day she was to leave the hospital.

"Mrs. Whitfield, I wanted to tell you about the baby.

"Just a few hours before her new parents came to take her home, I went down to the nursery. A really nice nurse agreed to let me sit in a little room there and hold my baby and have a last visit with her. It was so hard for me, but I still wanted to do it. I talked to her a lot and held her close. She was so little and cuddly. Then I gave her my last kiss. The nurse had to take her then and get her ready to go. (Elyse gained control of her voice.) It's all over now."

"Yes, it is Elyse, and you have done so well!"

The doctor allowed Elyse to come to school for just two brief visits. She had to rest at home until her blood pressure was within safe limits.

Her last visit was on Grace's day, and we all laughed together when Elyse said she had asked the doctor if she could skip taking the tranquilizer that morning so she could think clearly in the "group." The doctor had agreed.

It was a happy reunion for Elyse and Grace, and the girls enjoyed listening to Elyse as she told her story and finally brought it to a close with personal good-byes to each one. Elyse had asked her Grandpa to bring a camera when he came to pick her up. She asked Grace and me to come outdoors, and there she arranged herself between us and, with arms entwined, we stood together for a picture.

"Thanks, Grandpa, for taking the picture. I'll be ready in just a minute," Elyse called.

Grace had to leave. She and Elyse exchanged their good-byes. Then Elyse came over to me and said, "Thanks for everything, Mrs. Whitfield." I tried hard to keep smiling the whole time, but it wasn't easy. She had become a very special person, and it was hard to realize that she would leave us forever.

"Good-bye, Elyse. Take care. Have a good trip." I kept

saying all those automatic phrases, but they were helpful as I couldn't express my deepest feelings without tears.

After Elyse had gone, I sat thinking about her. I wondered what her thoughts and feelings and memories would be when she leafed through her album in the days and years to come and looked at the picture her Grandpa had taken of the three of us here at S.A.M.

CHAPTER 10

Ricky

I met Ricky for the first time the day that Jan (a new student) brought him in to "just talk." His face was reddened with anger, and the curly blond hair that touched his forehead was wet with perspiration. His eyes darted back and forth nervously. "I'm gonna take my car and crash it into the nearest brick wall. I don't care what happens to it or to me. I don't want to be in this mess, and I'll get out of it. You just watch me."

"You see, her parents called my parents and told them she's pregnant! So what am I supposed to do? Just stand there and take it. Boy, did my dad get pissed off at me. I'll be surprised if I even get back in my house again. They kept saying, 'So you went out and got a girl pregnant,' as if that's what I wanted to do! Oh shit, we were just having some fun after the concert. What does that have to do with a baby? I don't want to be a father.

"The talk around the gym was fun, checkin' out all the broads—who was doing what to who—which girls were easy makes. It was a game. Everyone was talkin' about how many times they scored and that if you weren't doin' it you weren't really macho. It really pisses me off how everyone talks about sex all the time. You got to perform or you're nothin'. Dammit! I don't want to be a father.

"It wasn't even fun. We were in the back of a friend's van and I was just wonderin' how much she would go for it. I had a half gallon of wine, and we both were feeling pretty good. So I put my arm around her shoulders and let my hand just brush across her nipples. I kept wondering how easy she'd be. She'd push my hand away and we would talk some more. It seemed like I kept checkin' for noises just in case someone might be coming. When it seemed safe I tried again. They say you got to take it easy with some girls. I told her I loved her and she believed me and we got it on. The moment that I had always heard about came almost like a mistake, and I thought—Oh my God! What have I done? Jan began to cry and shake in fear. She kept hanging around my neck. The van was like a prison, and there was no escape. I hated being there. I just wanted out. It was so awful and bad. Everything that I thought would be such a high became cheap and ugly. We just were trying to find out what everyone was talkin' about. I couldn't face her the next day, and at school she always looked down when I came by. We couldn't talk very well anymore and I guessed we should forget seeing each other.

"Jan came by a couple of months later saying she thought she might be pregnant. Oh my God! Why? The first thing I told her was have an abortion. They say that abortions are really easy now. A girl doesn't even have to go to the hospital a lot of the time. She can take care of the mistake without having to go to a lot of trouble. I told her I'd take her down to the clinic for her pregnancy test and to check out how to go about having the abortion.

"We waited in a hot waiting room. I looked around at the kids there and wondered if they were going through what

we were. It was the night for pregnancy testing and everyone looked scared and didn't say much. We had waited
over an hour when they called her. She got up slowly and
went in. As I watched her go, I kept wondering why the
hell I was even there? We didn't mean anything to each
other, and after it happened we both felt so guilty that it
was hard even to talk. Well, the test came out positive, and
I asked about the abortion. Jan didn't say much, but I could
tell she wasn't excited about the thought of it. Why should
she be so afraid of abortion? It was the only way.

"On the way home everything seemed so unreal and
strange. She told me she was afraid of abortion and we
argued. How could I know that her girlfriend had had an
abortion, and she told Jan about sitting on the toilet all
alone in some strange clinic and passing a bloody glob—
then flushing it down the drain. Jan couldn't do it.

"Well, the next thing I knew, her parents were calling
mine, and everybody was getting mad. My parents really
made everything a big hassle. The denied it at first, saying
that I wouldn't do anything like that. I heard them talkin'
from the other room. They were mad. Shit, was I in a bind!
Then I heard my dad sayin', 'We are going to have a talk
with Richard.' I felt like punchin' them out before they
could get to me. Well the 'talk' was really a lot of yelling
and things like, 'A kid your age doesn't get a girl pregnant.
It's different when you're in high school.' Mom kept sayin'
and cryin', "My little boy a father? Oh no, oh no.' They
wouldn't believe me when I said I didn't mean it. Dad kept
going on about things like paternity suits and child-support
payments. The whole evening was like that. I didn't think
I'd live through it.

"Then Jan tells me she's goin' through with the pregnancy and comin' here. God, everyone who looks at her
knows she's pregnant. She's ruining my life. I can't stand it

around here anymore. I'm quittin' school and takin' off. I don't care what happens. No one will find me and that's just fine." Ricky's car peeled out of the parking lot, leaving us stunned. It was the last Jan would see of him for a long time. She had heard from his friends that he had loaded his backpack and was hitching East. He had sold his car for living money and just took off. Nobody, not even his parents, knew where he was or where he was headed.

The months that brought Jan's pregnancy to term passed without any word from Ricky. She gave birth to a 6 lb. 12 oz. girl with her mother at her side. When she brought the baby back to school, I could see a resemblance to Ricky in the baby's face. Jan was still hurt and angered by Ricky's leaving, but she was determined to raise the child as best she could whether he was around or not. It was her mistake too, and she would face up to it by doing the best she could. She was so determined, it was almost as if she were punishing herself.

One day when the baby was about 3 months old, Ricky appeared. No one even knew he was in town, and he wanted it that way. He had come to see his baby. The safest place to do that was at S.A.M. He waited outside in the distance to see if Jan got off the school bus. When he saw her come in, he followed. "Jan, Jan," he called softly. She was startled by his voice. At first she just stared at him, not believing her eyes. Ricky's blond hair was long and matted against his head. He had a reddish scraggly beard, and he was very thin. His clothes smelled like the months on the road. Jan just stared into his haunted eyes. "I came to see the baby. My God, she's little!" Ricky looked around him quickly. "Don't tell anyone I'm in town. I'm just passing through on my way north to do some pickin' in the fields up there. It's the season, you know."

"No, I didn't know—is that what you've been doing mostly?"

"At first I hit the road and hitched across most of the country. I met up with some other guys who were doin' like me, only they were runnin' from the law...She's really so little...I just didn't imagine she'd be so little. It's so strange she's even here at all, us not even thinkin' about a kid and all.

"That night seems so long ago. If we could just go back in time and change everything. Then I wouldn't be runnin', and you wouldn't be a mother havin' to take care of a kid before your time. Just seein' her and you together looks so strange—like things are in the wrong time and place. I've got to go, you know—up north to the fields."

"Here Ricky, you hold her for a minute." Jan put the tiny bundle into Ricky's reluctant and shaking hands. His thin arms awkwardly encompassed the baby, and he gazed into her small face for a moment and then gave her back to Jan.

"You know pickin' time starts this month and I want to get on the crew. I can't waste time." Then Ricky spoke with an inward look. "This time away for me has been hell. It just seemed best to be away for a while—kind of to settle the air, you know, to have some thinkin' time—sorta to know what to do and all. I've been doin' a *hell* of a lot of thinkin'. Wishin' doesn't make it go away. The same thing keeps hittin' me between the eyes again and again....You can't run away from bein' a father. That kid bein' here and all—I'm her father forever and ever. No matter how far away I am, I'm still her father. No matter who you marry, I'm still her father. No matter what I do, I'm still her father!"

Then Ricky reached down for the pack at his feet and

heaved it up on his shoulders. He turned and walked out slowly with his heavy load. He plodded down the road in the direction of the freeway. His thumb weakly motioned to the passing traffic. A van stopped, the door closed behind him, and he was gone.

CHAPTER 11

Cecille

ecille was beautiful. She stood tall with a slender, feminine grace. A cloud of black hair softly framed her face. Her dark eyes, winged eyebrows, smooth lustrous skin, and full red lips made it hard to take your eyes from her face.

Her manner was aloof, sophisticated, and seemingly unrelated to the reality of her situation, which was one of violence and ugliness.

Cecille was sixteen, but she looked twenty-one. She came to S.A.M. because her defenses were crumbling.

No one knew of her pregnancy, which was caused during one night of terror.

As Cecille related the story, Dominic was a young man who came to work at the car assembly plant where her dad worked. Dominic lived in an apartment house some distance away from the plant in the opposite direction from her dad's house.

One evening Cecille's dad told the family that this kid from his plant was going to come to the house that night. He was from the East, her dad said, and didn't have any family out here.

Dominic came by about an hour later and met all the family, and sat around talking to her dad and drinking beer with him most of the evening.

This same kind of visit occurred about twice a month, and a couple of times Dominic had dinner at their house.

On one of these evenings, Dominic said he was going to the store to get ice cream and also to get gasoline and oil for his car at a service station. Dominic insisted that Cecille ride along with him to the store. "Go on, Ceci," her dad urged. Once in the car, she became frightened when she noticed he turned in the opposite direction from the ice cream store. Dominic headed toward the freeway construction site, which was deserted at that time of night. He pulled the car over close by some thick hedges that had not yet been bulldozed for the roadbed. He told Cecille to get out of the car. When she asked why, he took her arm and roughly pushed her out the door and over to the bushes. He told Cecille she had driven him crazy the last months, and he wanted to make love to her. He accused her of leading him on, the way she walked and acted. Then he told her she was very beautiful. Cecille, confused, frightened, and embarrassed, protested strongly. Dominic pulled a knife from his jacket and warned her not to make any sound or try to get away. He also warned her to say nothing about this to her parents or she could expect worse things to happen.

"It was so gross," Cecille said, "I was crying all the time. A rock was hurting my head and I felt his fingers digging into my flesh. I was sickened by the smell of beer on his breath as his mouth kept smothering me. This sweaty guy was hurting me so bad!"

My urge, as I heard Cecille speak, was to cry out in horror and disbelief. How, to this day, can children like Cecille be intimidated, shamed, and then made to feel guilty, that somehow they are responsible for the crime committed against them?

I remained silent. This was not the time or place to vent my feelings. Cecille had come here because she was looking for help.

She said she thought she was in the eighth month. She did not appear pregnant at all. Her posture was perfect. The blue jeans tightly zipped across a gently rounded tummy did not give her secret away. A color-matched cardigan, layered precisely over a soft, blue silk striped blouse, completed her well-groomed look.

At the high school, the nurse had observed Cecille hanging around the hall outside her office. She had decided to try talking to her in private and offering her help.

Cecille responded. She acknowledged her pregnancy but had no idea what she was going to do. She was determined that no one must know; she would have the baby and then leave it wherever she had it.

The nurse saw how troubled this girl really was and how desperately she needed help, and she agreed. She was knowledgeable enough to realize that her fantasy about leaving the baby when it was born was just that. But she was frightened, too. It was all beginning to close in around her. Cecille agreed to ride over to S. A. M. with the nurse a few minutes later.

Sitting across from me at a table, Cecille was wide-eyed and intense, yet trying to maintain a cool, detached manner as she asked me question after question—"When do I expect the baby? How will I know? What should I do? Will it hurt a lot?"

Four weeks to prepare for childbirth! This beautiful girl. This victim. How could I keep my feelings down? Anger flooded my thoughts. Yet, never, never would I betray my feelings. I knew that we must make every moment of Cecille's time at S.A.M. count! So much to learn just to prepare for a successful childbirth experience. All the other things, so important in the growth of S.A.M. girls, would have to be pushed aside for now, at least.

I offered to arrange for Cecille to get an appointment with a doctor right away. She was gratefully relieved. Following the doctor's appointment two days later, Cecille reported that the birthdate was set as two weeks away! I caught my breath. I had thought four weeks was not enough time! One of the first tasks facing Cecille was to tell her mother. I talked with her about this right away. She was very fearful of her mother's anger. I explained that anger often was the first reaction, but that most mothers settled down after they got over the shock of their daughter's pregnancy. She could have a friend go with her—the nurse or I would go if she needed us. Then Cecille said with confidence, "Yes, I will tell her I'm pregnant, but I will never tell her who did it! I am going to have to move out anyway. I can't live there anymore, worrying about when that creep Dominic might drop in again!"

I suggested that Cecille's mother might want to be with her during her labor and the birth. Cecille scoffed at the idea, saying, "She'll probably drive me to the hospital and dump me on the doorstep."

The next days were crowded with an intensive course in the practice for childbirth. One of the girls who had delivered worked with Cecille most of each morning helping with the relaxation techniques. In the afternoon I taught her about childbirth, signs of labor, stages of labor, and the delivery itself. She learned the breathing and began prenatal exercises.

Cecille's head must have been swimming, but her cool, quiet manner covered up her feelings.

One day she nearly broke down and put on a pretty

maternity top that was offered to her by one of the girls in school; Cecille was uncomfortable in her restricting clothes. She took the top home with her that day, but she never wore it. The next morning, Cecille called from the hospital. Her mother had taken her there at 5:00 A.M. She said she'd call us later on, but she didn't. That evening I called the hospital to inquire. Cecille had given birth to a baby boy at 3:30 P.M. I asked the nurse why I had not been connected with Cecille's room. The nurse said the doctor had given Cecille a sedative and that her calls were being received at the desk. I hung up the telephone feeling disturbed—this was not usual procedure. I told my family I was going to the hospital and would be back soon.

When I found Cecille's room, it was dimly lit and she was alone. I tiptoed over to the bed. Cecille was sleeping heavily. I watched her a few moments, but she never stirred. I felt comforted to see her. I took a piece of paper from my purse and wrote a note to her, propping it against the water glass on her bedstand. Then I left.

The next morning I waited again for the telephone to ring. The girls asked about Cecille, and I told them she had a little boy.

"Is she going to keep it?" Marie asked.

"I don't know," I answered, realizing that the same feeling of disturbance I had the night before was washing over me again. There had been so little time for Cecille, and we had not spent any of it talking about her plans for the baby. (Surely this could have been a child to give up for adoption, but no such arrangements had been discussed. The baby was here!)

Fortunately, the girls did not ask to telephone Cecille, as they so often did. I guessed they had not really gotten to know her in the two weeks that had flown by so fast.

I could hardly wait for school to be over that day, as I

knew I was going to head straight for the hospital.

The girls left, and as I hurried around straightening up, Michelle said, "Cathy, it's not hard to see that something's bothering you."

"I'm worried about Cecille," I told Michelle. Then I told her about the evening before.

"I feel so sorry for Cecille," Michelle said. "What chance does she have to make it now?"

Michelle's words haunted me as I drove toward the hospital. Before I was aware of what I was doing, I found myself again in Cecille's room. I smiled at her and she looked back at me with pain-filled eyes.

"So you had a little seven-pound boy! That's wonderful! How did it go for you?"

"It was awful," Cecille said. "I just couldn't do it. It hurt so much, I just was crying and screaming. I guess the doctor gave me a shot because I don't remember much else. A nurse came in this morning and said, 'Here's your baby.' So I guess I have a baby now to take care of..."

"Oh, Cecille," I thought, "you still cannot allow any true feelings to come out. . . . How terribly alone you are."

While still in the hospital, Cecille made arrangements to move in with an older girlfriend. So, from the hospital, she went to her friend's apartment. Her mother offered to help but Cecille refused, and her mother gave her some money instead.

Cecille returned to school two weeks later. She brought her dark-haired infant in and went to the nursery to lay him in a crib.

"Hey, Cecille, let us see your baby," shouted Anne. Cecille retraced her steps and put the baby down on the couch for everyone to see. Complimentary remarks came from the girls, and one wanted to pick the baby up. Cecille didn't seem to mind.

"What's his name?" Anne asked.

"Robert," Cecille replied. After the girls had finished looking at Robert, Cecille took him into the nursery and soon returned to the table where she had put her book bag and the baby's things. She took a baby bottle over to the refrigerator, placing it on one of the shelves. Then she came to my desk and began to talk about the schoolwork she needed to make up.

We talked about work for a while, and then I asked, "How are things going for you now?"

"O.K., I guess," Cecille replied. "I am going to get a job at one of those fancy waterfront restaurants in the evenings because I need a lot of money. My roommate says she'll stay with the baby at night, but I will pay her, too."

"That sounds like a good arrangement, Cecille," I said.

"My mother said she would help out too, if I needed her."

"I am glad to hear that you and your mom can be friends again." Cecille made no further comment.

Two group-discussion days had gone by with Cecille saying very little. Grace was allowing opportunity for Cecille to become involved without putting any pressure on her in the group. But Cecille was quiet. "Don't worry, Cathy," Grace said to me after one such session. "Cecille has been through a great deal of trauma these past months. It's not something she wants to talk about, and she's afraid to get into discussion for fear something will slip out that she must keep hidden for now. Let's just be glad that she is coming here each day and that she has a good job to keep her occupied and supplied with the money she needs for herself and the baby. Maybe, in time, we'll find Cecille will need our help much more."

One day Cecille did not show up at school. Several days passed, and still she had not returned. I decided to call her. When no one answered at the apartment, I called Cecille's parents' house. Cecille answered the phone. She sounded dull and far away.

"Hi, Cecille, have you been sick?" I asked.

"No," came her dull reply.

"Has the baby been sick?" I probed.

"No," Cecille answered again in the same faraway voice.

"Cecille, what is it; I'm worried about you," I pursued.

"Dominic came back. . . . He tried to. . . do it again. I hate him. . . I hate men."

"Oh, Cecille, how awful. I'm so sorry. Would it be all right with you if Mrs. Hartley came there to see you?"

"It's O.K., " Cecille agreed.

"All right then, I'll call her, and I'll talk to you later. Good-bye." When I hung up the phone my hands were shaking and my heart was pounding.

I called Grace to tell her about Cecille and that I had "volunteered" her for a home visit. Grace quickly agreed, saying, "Oh, Cathy, that poor child. How much more can she stand?" Grace left her office early that afternoon for Cecille's house.

Her mother opened the door and invited Grace in.

"Mrs. Ferrano, it's so nice to meet you. I am glad Cecille can be with you. She's been through so much."

"I'm so worried about Ceci. She doesn't want to talk or do anything. She just sits in a chair. I have to remind her to do things for the baby."

"She has had some experiences that have left her shocked and depressed. She's afraid to try anything right now. . . . She needs time and some help.

"I am going to talk with Cecille now. Do you suppose you could take care of the baby so Cecille won't be interrupted?"

"Oh, yes, I'll be glad to do that," Mrs. Ferrano replied.

"Thank you. I'll talk with you again after Cecille and I have talked."

Grace went into a small bedroom where Cecille was sitting in a rocking chair.

"Hello, Cecille. I wanted to visit with you a little while."

Cecille turned her head and said, "Hello, Mrs. Hartley."

Grace continued, "You've had some bad times. I wonder if you would just want to tell me about it?"

With a big sigh, Cecille started to tell the story of the night at the apartment.

"It was evening, and it was my night off from work. I was at home relaxing when my mother called me on the telephone." (I was to be a long time piecing together the whole story.)

"Dominic stopped by my parents' house and asked where I was living. He wanted to come by and visit me and see the baby.

"I told my mother I was really tired and would rather not have Dominic visit. My mom said, 'Cecille, you just don't have any social life or friends. Now, why don't you have a visit with Dominic, seeing he wants to see you so much?' I tried again to explain to my mom, but finally I gave up. I sat by the telephone a few minutes feeling scared and desperate. Jeanne, my roommate, was out for the evening.

"Dominic got there and looked around the apartment. (I guess he saw no one else was there.) He came over close to me saying, 'Baby, you're sure looking good. I've been thinking we should get married and be one big happy family.' Dominic was laughing in kind of a crazy way. He grabbed at me, ripping the buttons from my blouse. I tried to get away. I was hitting him but he kept hold of me.

"I was so scared and sick. I hated him.

"All of a sudden I knew what I was going to do. Almost casually, I picked up the long scissors from the counter and turned toward him and stabbed him. I saw blood coming out from the side of his neck and a look of pain on his face. I dropped the scissors and ran out of the apartment, knowing I had to get away from him."

Cecille then ran down the hallway and out the rear door. Once outside, she hid behind some shrubbery in front of a darkened apartment. She waited, listening for Dominic's footsteps, her heart pounding in her throat.

She bagan to get cold and cramped, but "I didn't dare move or make a sound." She thought she heard the baby crying, but she was afraid to go inside.

Finally, Cecille knew what she must do. Carefully, she slid along behind the shrubs until she reached the end of the apartment building. She could see Dominic's car still parked down the street. Staying out of the light, Cecille made her way to the second apartment house, where a girl she knew from high school lived with her parents. Cecille knocked on the door. Jenny's father opened the door, and Cecille asked if she could use their phone.

She dialed her parents' number and waited tensely for an answer. Fortunately, her mother answered. "Mom, I'm in awful trouble. Please, you and Dad come right over. Park down in front of Jenny's apartment house and I'll meet you at the car. Hurry, hurry, please," Cecille pleaded.

In minutes her folks were there. Cecille dashed out and jumped into the car. She blurted out the whole story. Her mother was in a state of shock, but her father jumped out of the car saying he was going to call the police. Cecille and her mother huddled together in the car. Minutes later, they heard Dominic's car start up, squeal into a sharp turn, and speed away.

When her father returned, the three of them went back to the apartment. The baby was lying on the floor screaming. Cecille's mother let out a cry and ran and picked him up. Deep red marks showed across his face. Cecille's mother was sobbing as she held the baby close to her and rocked him. She kept moaning and crying, "Oh my baby, my baby, my Ceci."

When the police arrived, Cecille's father gave them a description of Dominic and his car. Then he helped Cecille gather up some things she needed and, while she wrote a note for Jeanne, he put the things in the car. Cecille and her mother followed with the baby.

When Cecille was finished with her story, she just sat quietly, seeming to retreat again into a world that was safer and more comfortable to be in than the one she had just told Grace about.

"Oh, Cecille how sorry I am. How bad it's been for you!" After a while Grace said, "Cecille, the things that happened to you were not right and they were no part of anything that you did wrong. You were the victim of a man who has many problems. There will be policemen working to find him and protect other girls from him. I want you to begin to think about things you want to do for yourself, to make plans for some happy days ahead that you deserve to have. You know you have your whole life ahead of you."

"I don't know what they're going to do to me when they find out about the stabbing, but I had to do it."

"You have your mother and father who know what happened and who will stand up for you all the way—no matter what happens; and I know, and Mrs. Whitfield knows about Dominic, and we can all help if we're needed. But my guess is that you may never again see or hear of Dominic in this state. He probably got out right away so he wouldn't be caught here."

"Oh, that sounds good, Mrs. Hartley." Cecille smiled a little, for the first time.

"Well, good. I'm glad to see you smiling a little. Tomorrow afternoon I'll stop by again, to see you."

And so the days went on. A little at a time, Cecille began to think about herself, her life, and some goals she wanted to set about accomplishing.

By the time Grace brought up the subject of returning to S.A.M., Cecille had become quite strong and seemed confident enough to join the girls and be in school again. I had called, urging Cecille to come back. Grace told Cecille that nothing had been said at school about her experience, so she could return and make a fresh start.

Before the school year was over and she left S.A.M., Cecille was back at her job in the evening at a waterfront restaurant. The baby was cared for at home by her parents, who had become very supportive.

Cecille had one more year at high school before graduation. She planned to get her diploma and then complete a two-year course in health services. Her chosen career was one with challenge and potential for independence, which was so important to Cecille, who now was taking responsibility for herself and her baby.

CHAPTER 12

Mrs. Bennett

Mrs. Bennett was angry. She glared at her daughter, almost daring Lisa to speak.

It was my first meeting with Mrs. Bennett and Lisa, and my first task was to calm them both enough so that we could at least have a conversation.

Mrs. Bennett was a slim, attractive woman. She was well groomed. Only her tight lips and the deep furrow in her forehead told me she was a woman with the hardness it sometimes takes in this world to get along. She had been married twice, and Lisa was the product of the first marriage. She was young when she met Lisa's father—seventeen, and he was nineteen. They thought they were in love and had a fiery romance which resulted in Lisa's birth. They ran away to be married, never telling anyone that the pregnancy was already a reality. Lisa's father went from job to job, never finding anything that really satisfied him. Money was continuously a problem. He wanted to get away from the burden of wife and children and do something really exciting for a change. He was young and energetic. Why should he work hard each day and just go home and sit in front of the television?

At the same time, Lisa's mother felt trapped at home, not able to go on to school or work. She was unskilled and felt that she and Lisa should be cared for completely by her husband. She became apathetic, and the months turned into years. They hoped that maybe another baby would bring their faltering marriage back, but the new child just caused an additional financial burden and entrapment for them both.

When Lisa was five, their divorce became final. Mrs. Bennett looked for a job and a new husband to care for her children. These were hard years for Lisa. She had become so independent at such a young age. She remembered the fights and unhappiness. Everything she tried seemed to go wrong in her mother's eyes. Her mother was struggling to make a living at a factory job and had little time and patience to be with the children.

Lisa then saw a parade of her mother's boyfriends. She was aware, even though she was young, that her mother exchanged favors for gifts. Lisa wanted her mother for herself—she didn't want to share her with anyone. When Lisa was nine, Ed Bennett came into the picture. Lisa didn't particularly care for the man who was soon to be her stepfather, bus she could tolerate him better than most of the former boyfriends. He didn't tease her like the others had, and he sometimes gave her money for ice cream cones.

As time went by, Lisa's old feeling of hopelessness and anger increased. Anger from her parents' fights, her mother's divorce, the years of an absent mother, a mother who had to be shared with boyfriends, and now only a tolerable stepfather. She felt unloved and resentful. She was determined she would find love to make her happy, and when she found Doug, she lavished all her love on him. Her search for love resulted in pregnancy.

Mrs. Bennett and Lisa glared at each other there in the office. Lisa's chin quivered. She had already experienced so much. The years of her growing up were hard enough. How much more could one lonely girl take?

Lisa slumped in her chair. She cast her eyes downward. Her figure, except for her bulging stomach, was like her mother's. In fact, Lisa looked very much like her mother. She had the same eyes, nose, and mouth. The only notable difference, besides age, was the deep furrow in Mrs. Bennett's forehead. It was easy for me to imagine Mrs. Bennett in Lisa's place only seventeen years before.

Mrs. Bennett spoke, "I have tried to do the best for Lisa. I know that the divorce was hard on her, but I always tried to do my best, and this is the thanks I get. Where did I go wrong? This has been a big blow to the whole family. Ed, that's Lisa's stepfather, has tried to be reasonable, but how can you be reasonable when your stepdaughter's seventeen, unmarried, and pregnant. I don't know how we'll tell the rest of the family. Maybe this year we just won't get together for holidays. It will be a shock to my parents, but maybe that's the best. I just don't know what to do. I don't know if we should have Lisa marry this guy and at least make it respectable. What do you think? Or maybe a marriage right now would complicate things more. Well, that's up to Lisa; she is the one who is going to have to start finding some answers. Then there's money." Mrs. Bennett continued, hardly pausing, "It costs a lot of money to have a baby these days. Who's going to pay the bills? This boyfriend of hers probably won't hand over anything for medical bills. It's his baby, too, you know. We'll get stuck paying for this whole thing. And then, where will she stay while she's pregnant? I don't see how she can live at home and be pregnant. My God, everyone will know. She will have to stay inside—that's for sure. I suppose I could take her back and forth to S.A.M. in the car. It will help some as far as the neighbors go. But she will definitely have to stay inside. I've asked Lisa what she wants to do about the baby, and she says she wants to keep it! How can she mean that? She doesn't even know what it takes or what it costs to raise a baby. She doesn't even know how much she's going to have to give up in order to be a mother. It's not an easy thing to be a good mother. Sure, babies are cute, and it's fun to dress them up, but in a year or two they're hardly babies at all, and they *demand* your constant attention. You can hardly do anything without being with them or thinking about them. They say that a mother never has a peaceful night's sleep after her children are born. It's true; at first you're feeding them at all hours, then you're listening for them and covering them up. Then you sit up with them when they are sick or hear them coughing in the night. When you get past those years, you are up listening for the key in the lock and worrying if they are all right. How can she say that she wants to keep her baby? She doesn't know what it's all about!"

"Mrs. Bennett," I said with feeling, "you have so much on your mind right now. You and Lisa can't solve everything today. But you have time on your side. We have five months before the baby is born to think and work things through. You are welcome to come here any time and we can talk. You can only deal with one day at a time right now."

"Lisa hasn't been in school much since she became pregnant," Mrs. Bennett started again. "We thought she had an ulcer, so I took her to the doctor and he gave her some medicine for it (later we found out she was pregnant). She stayed home a lot, and I am afraid she is way behind in her schoolwork. Could she make up her work here?"

"Yes, she can; I am sure that it won't be long before she

is caught up. She can even work ahead if she wants to."

Mrs. Bennett looked around and then said, "I was afraid that this school would be for juvenile delinquents and dropouts. But everyone here looks pleasant, and your school is so cheerful. A person could really feel very comfortable here.' Turning to Lisa, she said, "Lisa, would you like to come to this school?"

"Yes, I think so," Lisa replied softly.

Lisa started on Monday. I provided her with the time and comforting words she seemed to need. At first she began to share her experiences with the others and found that she had many things in common with them. Soon she was involved with her schoolwork and making headway. In the following weeks, Mrs. Bennett came to school several times and we talked.

She talked about her feelings of being afraid she had been a poor mother, of the struggles she had had raising her children, how she was finding it so difficult to accept Lisa as she was. She had pictured her daughter having the things she had never had and being a success in life. It was her goal for Lisa to be successful and to be spared life's troubles such as she had experienced. Mrs. Bennett was disappointed and full despair. Now, all that she had wanted for Lisa was impossible.

Grace met with Mrs. Bennett for one long afternoon session. Mrs. Bennett poured out her confusion, despair, and disappointment a little at a time. Grace helped Mrs. Bennett to see and understand Lisa's frustrations as well as her own. Grace gently charged Mrs. Bennett with adult responsibility to help and support Lisa so that she could come through the time of her pregnancy with no further emotional damage and with every possibility of becoming better able to understand herself and learn more mature ways to cope with her problems. Mrs. Bennett expressed doubt that this could happen, but Grace reassured her. "The coming months at S.A.M. will be a time of great changes for Lisa. I feel sure that, with your help, good things will result for both you and Lisa. You know we want to think, after a while, about what Lisa's plans will be for the future—after the baby. She will hear about adoption at S.A.M., and she will have time to explore this option, so that when she makes her final decision about keeping or giving up her baby, she will feel she has made the best decision for her."

Mrs. Bennett sat quietly and listened now. Grace could see a faraway, thoughtful look in her eyes. Again, quietly, Grace suggested, "Sometimes our dreams for our children are really dreams for ourselves, and often they're not very realistic. It's hard to accept our children growing up and having their own values, opinions, and needs for independence. Now Lisa and you have an additional challenge, and it will be important to see how well you both can work things out."

By the time the school potluck dinner came around, both Mrs. Bennett and Lisa were more settled. Mrs. Bennett reported that even Ed was accepting things better.

I always enjoyed the potluck evening because it gave me a chance to meet the whole family of each girl and often the father of the baby. That night, each family brought in their favorite dish carefully wrapped with foil, and the aroma of the foods from the different cultures blended together to give an international flavor to the evening. A long table was specially set up to accommodate all the different dishes. Everyone was in a festive mood. Parents met each other for the first time and shared personal experiences. As the evening progressed and the young ones were asleep on their mothers' laps, I could sense, as we all did, a common bond of understanding. Parents who felt so alone and isolated in their problem could talk with other parents with mutual respect for what each had gone through. The families felt reassured that their daughters were getting help in coping with their pregnancies as well as getting a good education. Something *was* being done in our community for these girls rather than ignoring the many facets of the problem, hoping that with today's thinking and the pill, pregnancy would take care of itself. The potluck dinner was always a rewarding evening for me. By the time the last paper plates were disposed of and various ceramic and plastic bowls were washed, it was late in the evening when the last mothers emerged from the kitchen. When the parents had left, Michelle and I took off our shoes and reflected upon the evening. "The Bennetts sure looked good tonight," Michelle said. "Mrs. Bennett looked more relaxed than I have ever seen her. The magic of S.A.M. must be working."

Lisa was in her seventh month, and it was time for her to think of prepared childbirth classes. Her boyfriend became more and more distant. In fact, they hardly saw much of each other anymore. One day Lisa came to me with a very worried look. "Mrs. Whitfield, I don't have anyone to be with me during my labor and delivery. I don't want to be alone. What should I do?" she asked.

"Lisa, have you ever thought of asking your mother to be with you?"

"Oh, no, she would never do it."

"How do you really know if you don't ask her—you might be surprised."

"I'll think about it, Mrs. Whitfield."

Two weeks later, Mrs. Bennett and Lisa enrolled in childbirth classes. There was a notable difference in Lisa. She seemed more settled and content. The angry look in her eyes was gone. She needed her mother's help and was accepting it. Mrs. Bennett felt good in the ways she was able to help and to have the opportunity to help. Mother and daughter accepted each other's needs and respected each other's rights. A healthy relationship was sprouting.

The last two months flew by for Lisa and her mother. They had finished their classes and were awaiting the birth.

Lisa remained firm in her decision to keep her baby. Her mother became more accepting and began to buy baby things. The two decorated the corner of Lisa's bedroom that was to be the baby's nursery. The empty crib with its stuffed toys awaited the baby's arrival.

Mrs. Bennett called me early one morning with the news that Lisa was in labor and that they were leaving for the hospital. The girls were very excited and wondered, as each hour went by, how it was going for Lisa and her mother. "Let's call the hospital, Mrs. Whitfield," they would say.

"Lisa's mother promised she would call us as soon as she could," I assured them.

The school bus pulled up to the curb to take the girls home. They were very disappointed that we hadn't heard from the hospital. They were gathering their books when we were all startled by the telephone ringing. They rushed into the office to listen on the extension, repeating everything aloud to the girls whose ears weren't glued to the telephone. "It's a girl...8 pounds 3 ounces...went 'natural' the whole way...feels tired...20 hours of labor... her Mom was with her in the labor and delivery room... she held the baby...wow, that's great." By now the bus driver had come to the door and, hearing the news, she squealed with excitement with the rest of us.

Mrs. Bennett came with Lisa and the baby when Lisa returned to school three weeks later. While the girls were hovering over the new mother and child, Mrs. Bennett motioned to me to come into the office. She wanted to talk. I was unsure of what she wanted to say when we sat down. She began, and tears filled her eyes. "It was such a beautiful experience that Lisa and I shared during her labor and delivery. It was hard work, yet there were light moments. It was tough, yet it was rewarding. She cried out for me, and I was there to reassure her. It was everything our life together should have been before this whole thing happened. We have a special bond now that's hard to explain —it's like sharing a miracle together. Lisa and I had to go through all the anguish of her pregnancy and the miracle of her delivery to finally find and understand each other. What we have together now is something we will have forever."

Mrs. Bennett said good-bye and I walked over to the couch to look closely at the new baby girl for the first time. She was a beautiful baby and had Lisa's eyes, nose, and mouth. She looked just like Lisa except for a furrow in her forehead that reminded me of her grandmother.

CHAPTER 13

The First Year Ends

I t was spring and the school year was coming to a close. It meant the end of my close personal association with all the girls. They began expressing feelings of nostalgia about S.A.M., even though it had been only one school year. The group was so close now. How changed they seemed from the beginning of the school year. I thought back to how each girl entered with her individual dilemma, and how she moved from this central theme of dilemma to one of positive direction. From aloneness, crisis, and feelings of inferiority, the girls, over the period of their time at S.A.M., learned that they were human beings deserving of respect and obligated to develop themselves according to their own abilities so that they could become all that they had the potential to be.

In the beginning, each girl was separate from the rest, bringing with her just her own background and experiences. But as time passed for her, she became a part of something greater than herself. In a climate of comfort and caring, she lost her fears of failure and aloneness. She was supported in her efforts to complete her schooling by close personal contact with the teacher. Her individual class program was designed for success. Progress was the only outcome. She became more confident and more successful.

Through improved communication skills, the group began to express their views to each other on many subjects. When conflicts arose, they took readily to democratic principles and were willing to discuss their differences and accept the decisions they made as a group.

They started school afraid that the girls might be cliquish and that they might feel left out. Yet before long they came to know and feel that respect was part of S.A.M. Each person was entitled to respect and to be respected.

I began preparing each girl for the separation that the close of school and summertime would bring. The preparation involved appreciating the past but, most of all, looking toward the future.

When one or another of the girls would say, "I just don't know what I'm going to do without S.A.M.," I would sit down with her again and go over the directions and choices she might take. We'd talk about making new friends, the rewards of working in a good job, and, for some, the possibilities of college. I would hope I had reassured her so that she could begin seeing herself separated from us. It was always understood that any day, any time, the girls could come back to visit and talk.

I didn't want anyone to have the feeling that she wasn't supported. We would always make ourselves available.

Grace came for her last visit, and the girls wanted to talk about what the year had meant to them.

Lisa began first. "It's a second home at S.A.M. I've spent all my days here since last October. Before I came, I was confused. I was worried about being out of school and getting behind. I was a disappointment to my mother. I didn't know anything about childbirth or babies. When I first came, I was quiet and scared. I felt alone, but I soon realized that everyone was so helpful and was going through a lot of the same things, and that gave me more confidence."

Cecille added, "And most important, there are loving people here who care about and help you. There should be more people like that in the world. I enjoy being myself. I'm understanding more, and I like myself better."

From time to time, Grace and I exchanged glances. We were overwhelmed by the outpouring of feelings. It was as if each girl needed to tell her story to be at peace about leaving. Back and forth they went, talking about all their experiences at school.

"I wanted to graduate," Alicia began. "Everyone, including me, thought it was impossible, but I have made it. I will graduate this June. Now my baby won't have a drop-out for a mother.... That makes me feel like a better person and a better mother."

"Next semester, when I return to my high school," Elyse added, "I will still be where I should be, and this time away won't have put me behind."

Mauvine chimed in. "I used to hate school, but now I know I can make it there, and in a year I'll be graduating."

When they were satisfied with one topic, they put it aside to go on to another. Soon there wasn't a dry eye among us, and the tears carried our complete feelings. When the eyes were mopped, everyone felt better. When Grace got up to leve, she expressed her happiness at having been a part of the group. The girls poured out their "thank you's."

Now it was the last day, and it began as usual with the squeal of brakes from the big yellow school bus. Michelle said, "Well, this is it—after today summer vacation will be a different life for us."

"Yes, I know—we have become so much a part of

S.A.M. It is going to be a strange feeling not to be constantly thinking about each girl and seeing them each day. There's going to be a real emptiness."

The door opened, and the girls entered for the last time. The babies were put in their cribs, amd Michelle gave each girl a memory book that she had made. There were pages of poetry and humorous anecdotes, but the page that they liked the most was the autograph page. Books were exchanged and the girls wrote parting notes.

I assembled the report cards and talked with each girl personally as I gave them out, congratulating the high-school graduates and commending the school progress of those returning to regular high school. It was our last chance to talk. "I'll be back to see you, Mrs. Whitfield, you can count on that," was the sentiment many of the girls expressed. I secretly hoped that they would be back so I could know how they were doing. The girls could see my emotions building as the day progressed, and it was their turn to comfort me. Some of the mothers and boyfriends dropped by to say their good-byes. When it became obvious that the group could stay no longer, we reached out, hugging and crying our "good-byes."

As the bus pulled away, I knew that it would never be the same again at S.A.M. This first year would be etched in my mind forever—a year of changes, poignant moments, dramatic life stories and their outcomes.

I am alone now, and it is so very quiet. Only the echoes of the voices linger in my mind. I walked to the nursery half expecting to see the babies there, but the cribs were all empty. The music boxes were silent and the rocking chair was still. It was so quiet that the silence hung heavily around me.

In the main room I passed by the tables, picturing them covered with books and papers and busy girls sitting around them. Now they were vacant. I straightened a chair and pushed another in to the table, not really seeing what I was doing. Then I walked to the couch and sat down to gather my thoughts. I looked up and half expected to see writing on the blackboard, but it was erased cleanly. The school was so unreal now. Its life was gone. Here I had sat just ten months before wondering what the school would bring, and now not really believing it had ended.

While sitting on the couch, I could almost hear the voices of the girls as they had talked here with Grace:

Julie's crying spells as she decided about her baby still echoed in my ears. Mauvine, with her earthy approach to life, seemed to be sitting beside me. Frail Alicia's grasping for emotional stability tugged at me. Sandi laughed as she joked with the girls, and Alexandria fretted about her restrictive life now. Darlene's chronic unhappiness brought back that feeling of unrest to my mind. Elyse's innocence and brightness guided the group to achieving more than we thought possible.

They all seemed so close there, but, almost like a balloon bursting, I came back to the reality that I was sitting alone. My thoughts couldn't break the silence for long. I realized how much had happened during this one special school year:

Joe's concern about Rita during her labor flashed across my mind. And Cecille, were the scars of her tragedy lessening? I thought, too, of Ricky, so far from the child he had fathered. And the parents, all the parents like Mrs. Bennett, who face the shock and crisis of their daughter's pregnancy; how I felt for them!

It would take so many more days, weeks, so much more time to pass before I could feel recovered from the depth of my immersion in S.A.M. I was unaware of my body. Only my thoughts had reality. My consciousness was consumed with vivid thoughts of each one.

A lump in my throat was my first awareness of physical existence again. It rose higher in my throat and swelled until I was conscious of pain.

I couldn't stay a minute longer. With eyes blurred, I fumbled for my keys. Still lost in thought, I locked the heavy door.

CHAPTER 14

Time Passes

The years ran their course at S.A.M. Enrolling students brought their crises, life dilemmas, and struggles for solutions. Graduating students ventured forth with new awareness, self-esteem, and direction. Some students dropped out, falling into chasms of no hope and no future. Other students endured on the borderline of survival in a mire of complicated circumstances.

As a teacher, I struggled with a way of coping with daily difficulties and crises. I began to learn how to conserve my strength in order to retain my sensitivity. I learned that people have the right to fail as well as succeed. I grew along with my students—and because of my students.

The one thing that remained constant through the years were my students. Certainly the details of their stories varied, but their emotional states, the decisions they faced, the impact of pregnancy on their futures, the working through of relationships with parents and the baby's father continued to be the same. The stories of my first students are as valid today as when they were first written. The only difference is that today my students were younger in years.

Each year S.A.M. had a reunion. All the former students and their friends, husbands/boyfriends, parents, and children were invited. At first these reunions were small affairs held at the school, but by the time the tenth year rolled around it was evident that the event would have to be moved outdoors to the local park.

This potluck picnic in the park became *the* event of the school year. Invitations were sent out, but each year some were returned "Addressee unknown" or "Moved—no forwarding address." I was saddened to lose touch with these students. Others responded with long telephone conversations bringing me up to date on their situations. "Reunion time" each year became the time when students voluntarily touched base with S.A.M.

At the yearly picnic some of these young women brought husbands to be introduced, new boyfriends to show off, new babies to be admired. Their stories were told through their conversations, but many showed in their faces as well. The young girls I had known in class had grown up and were now in their late twenties or early thirties. The experiences of the years were often apparent in their eyes and faces; some faces were old and disheartened, others bright with interest and expectation.

My contact with former students was not exclusively at reunion time. Throughout the school year I never knew when the telephone would ring, a letter arrive, or the door burst open bringing a desire to show off a success or a need to discuss a problem. Some students kept in regular contact; others disappeared and then after years were rediscovered. Some were never heard from again.

From the original group of S.A.M. students whose stories we have told, we have chosen five to follow up as we were most current on their outcomes.

The stories of Alexandria, Cecille, Julie, Darlene, and

Joe show the life changes that occurred during the fifteen years between their attendance as pregnant teenagers at S.A.M. and their lives as they have unfolded to the present.

CHAPTER 15

Time Passes:

Alexandria

T he story of Alex began unfolding slowly at first with her initial stay with her aunt and her parents' continued involvement in her life. She wanted out from their control. She felt trapped.

She had a new boyfriend, Chuck, and the two of them talked about taking off for northern California to make a new life. Chuck had a married friend up there who he knew would put them up until they could get a place of their own.

Alex was happy at the thought of being free of her mother's judgment and free to raise little Diedre the way she wanted. Chuck was happy to have a girl like Alex to join him in a new adventure.

But it was difficult starting out in a strange city, with little money, and the friend's wife resenting them.

Even though Alex seemed to hate her parents, as time passed she missed them and longed to go home. She knew that was impossible, but nonetheless she wanted her mother as she faced caring for her baby without emotional support. Chuck couldn't understand how Alex could both hate and long for her mother.

Chuck was pressured for money, but he soon found a job as a construction worker. It was hard work and sporadic, and he was never able to get ahead. He often came home angry and resentful seeing Alex "just sitting around the apartment" caring for the baby. The rebellious spirit they had once shared became stifled by the pressures of survival.

School for either of them was an impossibility. It was clear that Alex had to find work as well, even though most of her paycheck would go to a baby-sitter for Diedre.

After three years of poverty and screaming fights over just about everything, Chuck met a man at work who seemed to have the answer, a way out. It was cocaine. It was free to try at first, of course; but the man said that if Chuck were clever and sold it, he could not only support his fun but Alex and Diedre as well. Chuck loved the relief of the high and went about learning what he needed to know to deal drugs. This was a quick fix to all their problems. But of course he wouldn't be doing it for long —just until they were on their feet.

Alex felt wrong about the whole arrangement, but for the first time in over three years they had money. They moved to a place of their own, bought a car, and for the next year and a half everything went well. She became pregnant and had her second child, Jason. Chuck was happy to have this little son of his own.

But Alex hated what Chuck was doing. He was being changed by drugs. At one point she felt that the old life, difficult as it was, at least was less worrisome.

One evening Chuck was late getting home. It was usual for him to deal at night, but Alex always felt nervous. Finally from her second-story window she saw his car drive up. She breathed a sigh of relief and turned away to greet him when the noise of a scuffle on the street below brought her back to the window. She saw one man holding Chuck, face down, on the sidewalk and the other looking through his car. She ran down the stairs two at a time thinking she could intervene. "Stay back, lady," the heavyset man holding Chuck yelled to Alex, "this man is under arrest."

Chuck's arrest, subsequent conviction, and jail sentence brought poverty back as a reality to Alex and her two children. She was loyal to Chuck at first and visited him in jail each week. But Chuck's sentence seemed so long, and as things became desperate she lost sight of their relationship. She began talking to Robert, one of the other inmates who had noticed her and spoken to her each week. It turned out that he was soon to be released.

As soon as Robert was free, he came to find Alex and ask if he could move in with her. Their affair was wonderful and seemed to solve many problems. As soon as he found work, Alexandria had someone to take care of her and her two children.

Alex wasn't certain of Robert's past but was willing to let him start over, which was fair, she thought. Alex wasn't upset when she became pregnant again. Back of it all she felt the pregnancy was a sure way of tying Robert to her.

But Robert wasn't as devoted as Chuck, and her pregnancy almost caused the end of their relationship. Alex persuaded Robert to stay with her, using the same charm he had seen in her during her visits to jail. When their baby boy was born she named him Robert Jr., and she conned Robert into marrying her.

Marriage was best, she privately told herself. Her children were five and two years, and now with little Robert to consider, they needed the stability of marriage.

During the next five years Robert gradually reverted to

old habits. Alex was not aware of this at first, but when things appeared around the house that she knew they couldn't afford, she suspected the truth and faced Robert with it. Out of his frustration at being confronted by Alex, he hit her. He promised he would never do it again, but after that whenever he reached the breaking point he hit her again and again.

Feeling responsible for the beatings, Alex looked for a way out and started drinking. One afternoon she awoke from a drunken stupor to the noise of her children fighting. She began to scream and scream and scream.

Here she was, twenty-five years old, three kids out of control, a husband who was no good, the father of another of her kids in jail, and nothing but emptiness and despair ahead. It was not hard to contemplate ending her life. But in her subconscious mind words surfaced that had been said to her when she was a pregnant student ten years before—"Don't lose heart, Alex, you have all that you need inside you to succeed."

"They believed in me then; why don't I believe in myself now?" Alex sobbed to herself.

Although hidden at first, the courage and effort she needed were there, and she called her parents. At first her mother was shocked, then overjoyed to hear from her. It had been so long that they had begun to wonder if she were alive or dead. Her father wisely avoided condemning her. As Alex seemed genuinely committed to getting back on her feet, he offered to take the children. Time and experience had changed both Alex and her parents. Her mother had learned that no amount of social standing was worth the loss of her daughter. With her mother's acceptance, Alex blossomed.

"That was five years age, Mrs. Whitfield. I'm thirty now,

divorced, and Diedre is fifteen, Jason thirteen, and Robert ten."

"Can they be that old?" I exclaimed. "It seems only yesterday you were here at S.A.M."

"I want to tell you what has happened. I haven't had a drink in five years!" Alex said, proudly continuing her story. Her parents had cared for the children while Alex recovered in a rehabilitation center. Then she went to an adult school, earned her diploma, and began a business program at college. She was calling to say she was graduating. Would I like to come to her graduation?

"I'd love to, Alex. In fact, I'd be honored."

I'm glad you never lost heart, Alex. I never doubted it. I knew you had everything you needed within you to work things out—to succeed.

CHAPTER 16

Time Passes: Cecille

Dear Mrs. Whitfield:

I wanted to see you one last time. It's been a real long time, I know. I'm not sure you even remember me or that you are still at S.A.M. I wonder, is the school still going? Do you ever see any of the other girls from my class? It seems I've lost track of everyone.

My son is fifteen now and in high school. Mom and Dad have raised him. At first it just seemed best, and they wanted to do it. Now he thinks of them as his parents, and I don't want to change that.

It probably seems strange that I'm writing to you, but I didn't know if you'd be there and I wanted to see you one last time. Call me if you receive this letter.

Sincerely,
Ceci

Cecille had written her telephone number in such a weak scrawl that I felt concerned in addition to the first feelings of surprise that overcame me as I opened her unexpected letter.

I reread the letter, speculating about the missing pieces of her life from the time when she finished S.A.M. to the present.

Her traumatic experience still gave me a chill as I recalled gruesome details of Cecille's rape by Dominic, who had been a friend of the family. I wondered how she had coped with her life after that horror.

I called Ceci the next day, and she was delighted. "The letter was the only way I could think of to reach you. I hoped it would be forwarded to you if S.A.M. was no longer there," she explained in a mature, rather heavy voice that had few of the inflections I remembered.

"How are you?" I inquired. "Oh, that's a long story," she sighed. "I was thinking back over my life, and I thought of S.A.M. For all my troubles at that time, I always felt I could talk to you guys." "You still can, you know," I responded. With this invitation, Cecille began her story, needing to spill out all the feelings she had held back over the years.

After S.A.M. and graduation she had continued her job at the Newport Beach waterfront restaurant. Her parents took over the responsibilities of her baby, feeling that this would help her to reestablish herself and earn her own money. They loved their little grandson and seemed able to block out the reality of his conception by seeing his innocence beyond any tie to Dominic. Ceci, however, found thoughts of Dominic hard to repress even though she had neither seen nor heard from him again. She imagined he had moved away from California, but her hatred and revulsion remained.

I knew the restaurant where Ceci worked. The waitresses wore skimpy nautical costumes, and I could imagine Ceci looking stunning as she moved among the tables in the course of an evening's work. I remembered her as a very attractive girl. Men would notice her face and figure. But she explained that she kept her distance because of her uneasy feeling about men.

As time went by, subtle changes took place in her as older, wealthy men offered her a life-style she had never had but was somewhat curious about. When she accepted Ron's invitation to spend a weekend on his boat, she was scared at first. But his affluence and mature ways appealed to her, and underneath it all she felt a need to make up for a lot. She had promised herself she would never have anything to do with a man again, but with Ron, instead of feeling threatened, she felt she had power. He was the one who was lavishing attention on her, who was weak and unable to be without her. She could live without men, but his gifts and invitations told her he could not be without women.

That first night on his boat she pretended her way through their intimacies. For that special weekend she had a yacht, a stateroom, and a sail on the Pacific—and he had her, so he thought.

After Ron, there were many others. Ceci became skilled at having no feelings. She liked what men could provide for her. She had expensive gifts, money, and an exciting Newport Beach life-style. What could be better?

She saw other women of her own age tied to children, work, and husbands. They might as well be middle-aged, she thought. She rationalized that her life-style was just getting back some of what Dominic had taken away.

Our conversation had gone on well over an hour at this point, and Ceci sounded tired. I suggested that we meet, together with Mrs. Hartley. "Oh, I'd love to see you both again," Ceci responded, as her voice perked up. "How about Saturday at the park where we had the reunions?" I suggested. "That would be wonderful! I'll see you there."

I called Grace, and she changed her Saturday tennis match so we could meet with Ceci. Grace had retired from S.A.M. and the school district but continued to make the most of her free time. She kept involved in her field through part-time work at the community college. She was surprised and delighted to hear about Cecille. I told her about my conversation with Ceci, and we speculated about our get-together.

At the park, sitting alone at a picnic table in the distance was a slender figure. We both recognized the dark hair and surmised this was Ceci. As we approached only a hint of the girl we knew showed in the skeleton-like face that was Cecille's. Her appearance, gaunt in repose, brightened with her recognition of us. "Mrs. Hartley. Mrs. Whitfield. I am so glad you have come. I've needed to talk to you. It's so good to see you again!" Grace and I disguised our shock at her appearance by showing exuberance at being together again.

Almost as if Cecille had planned and practiced her words for some time, she continued her life's story.

The high-style life in Newport Beach continued for some time, but as Cecille grew older her contacts became fewer and her income considerably less.

She decided to move to Los Angeles where living would be cheaper and she could perhaps get a job. She took a six-month business course and found a job as a receptionist for a real estate office.

Her new life wasn't at all what she had expected. She worked nine hours a day, made a third of her former income, had to deal with bills and payments. Her apartment was shoddy, and as she described it, her life was boring.

When she could stand the office work no longer, she went back to try again to get what she could from men. She found it took more effort to put herself together. She was competing with younger women in the bar scene, but she found it hard to admit she wasn't doing very well. Her clientele was different, and her standards changed. The places in Hollywood where she ended up looking for contacts were filthy and run down.

"It was awful, Mrs. Hartley, you wouldn't believe how bad it was. After a couple of years, I began to feel tired all the time. I kept losing weight. At first I thought it was wonderful not to have to watch my weight all the time. But then I realized I couldn't gain weight. Food made me sick to my stomach.

"Six months ago I went to a clinic in L.A. They took blood and checked me all over. I'm supposed to take these pills." Ceci reached into her purse and pulled out a large plastic bottle half filled with capsules. "I know there's no cure for AIDS, but maybe I'll be a medical breakthrough." she quipped, covering the sting of her true feelings.

Grace and I sat there chilled to the bone in the balmy California breeze and tried our best to change the unchangeable, to console the unconsolable, to somehow make things new again. But futile means futile. Reality is defined by reality, and there was nothing we could say or do.

"I wanted to see you again so I could go over everything out loud," Ceci continued, "...so it didn't have to be hidden any more...so I could have some peace. I feel better now...it's all over."

And there it all was in a flashback: rape, revenge, remorse.

CHAPTER 17

Time Passes: Julie

From time to time I had contact with Julie. She would call to share a thought or visit to see the babies at school. Each time we were together the struggle over her adoption decision was visible in her.

She told me about the day she went to the agency to relinquish her baby. She signed the forms setting in motion the legal adoption procedures. But she wanted and needed to be with her son one last time to say good-bye. The adoption worker brought him to her. As she sat clinging to her tiny child there in the agency waiting room, she whispered to him as she rocked him in her arms. She told him about his new parents and how excited they must be. Although she didn't know who they were, she knew they would have to be excited. This baby was so special, so beautiful. She told him he was getting a chance at a life she couldn't provide. But as she whispered the words, in her heart she believed she could be a good mother. She had loved him from the minute she had felt him move within her. Her deeply committed love for him could have carried them through any difficult time as long as they were together. Her tears fell like a baptism onto her sleeping

infant's head. She smoothed his hair as she tried to re-
concile herself to what she must do. But there was no
reconciliation as she went through the motions of wrapping
the baby in the new blanket her mother had lovingly knit-
ted. She got up slowly and walked to the adoption worker.
She exchanged all she had ever had of real meaning in her
short sixteen years of life for an indescribable emptiness.
She took from her purse the bundle of letters she'd written
to her firstborn. They were tied together with a ribbon. All
her thoughts and emotions were contained inside. She
handed them over as well, asking that the baby be given
the letters when he was old enough to understand. They
were to help him know how much she loved him, but he
could never really know in a lifetime about her grief of that
moment.

I didn't see Julie for some time. She decided to go to a
different high school from the one she had attended before
S.A.M. She felt it would be easier to start over. She told no
one about the pregnancy and adoption.

At first she and the baby's father were close, but because
they were attending different high schools their contacts
became less frequent. She didn't want to go to Steve's
senior prom because it would put her back among people
who might ask questions. It was best, she decided, never
to go back; it made it easier to forget. So Julie and Steve
saw less and less of each other as they separately worked
through their thoughts and feelings about their baby.

At her new school Julie made friends slowly. She was
quiet and preoccupied, which others misunderstood. High
school girls, who are by definition caught up in adolescent
thoughts of dates, clothes, and parties, couldn't possibly
understand Julie's grief about her baby, or so Julie believed. Her remaining school years were troubled. She
wrote more letters and poured out her heart in the pages.

Dear Baby,

You're one year old today. I wonder if you're walking or maybe saying "Mama." You can't possibly know how I miss you. I feel so empty and alone. I miss you being so close to me. At school no one knows; it's as if they are in another world from mine. They haven't been changed by difficult thoughts as I have. They seem so young. It's as if they are still children, and I'm grown up. I can't talk to them because they are so different from me. Baby, I need the strength to live through this.

When you were just born I knew exactly what I must do—give you up. But now I wonder if I did the right thing. Sometimes I feel regretful. Is it possible I could have regretted keeping you?

Mom says I should keep busy with new things that I enjoy doing, but it's hard enjoying anything. I keep thinking I'll see you at the market or in a stroller somewhere, but I know I'm just making it harder on myself by searching for you.

Be a good boy. Love,

Mom

Months passed and Julie battled her grief, but occasionally she had brighter moments like when her baby had his second birthday.

Happy Birthday, Baby!

Two years old. Imagine that. Two years old. I'm happy for you that you have your family and are probably having a birthday party. I wish I could be there too—not to interfere, of course, but just to see you. I could pretend I was a distant relative and could drop by, give you presents, and a big hug and *see* you again. I can imagine you are a big strong boy—you felt like one when we were together.

I will always remember your birthday. It is the most special day of the year.

Love your parents and be good.

Mom

After graduation Julie entered community college. She knew she wanted to work with young children, so she majored in preschool education.

At first she spent a great deal of time in the day-care nursery, holding and rocking the babies. But in time she became engrossed with her studies and didn't have the tugging of her thoughts. She was feeling some freedom. She knew through her experiences at the nursery what young mothers had to cope with—baby care, money, school pressures, home pressures, and many more. She realized she was more in control of her life now. She could make choices without having to consider the pressures she saw in the young mothers at the day-care center. Julie was wise beyond her years.

Another person came to play a role in Julie's life. A guy in her English class began to notice her. She was self-conscious and cool, and she kept the relationship at the friendship level, concealing her feelings as well as her thoughts. Nevertheless she enjoyed Doug's company, and he seemed to have no expectations about their friendship. They often had coffee or lunch together at school and met for talks between classes. Their relationship was unhurried.

Doug was making plans to attend the university about the time of Julie's baby's third birthday.

Dear three-year-old,

The thought of you being my child and then not being my child is torture to me. I never knew that the right decision would be so painful. Am I never to know you? I seem to suffer so much with my thoughts. I have a boyfriend at school, and I wish I could tell him about you, but I know I never can. I've told no one, and I could never tell a guy.

I want to wish you a happy birthday, three-year-old. I might be that stranger who comes to your party unannounced and showers you with hugs and kisses and presents and then goes off, not to be seen or heard from for another year! I love you forever.

Mom

Julie made it through her second year at college and planned to go on to the university. She changed her major to elementary education with the intention of becoming a teacher. She spent little time now in the day-care center, consoling herself that she never would have had the opportunities she now had if she hadn't made the right decision about the baby. A person could have regrets no matter what her decision.

She was accepted at a university in Santa Barbara, some distance from home. It would mean breaking away from family and old associations. Though they would miss her, her parents were glad for her.

She moved into a dormitory. She made new friends and became more social. Her girlfriends in the dorm liked her, and she felt freer than she ever had in her life. But she was never free enough to talk about her baby. That was still a deeply hidden secret.

One afternoon, some six weeks after the beginning of the

term, Julie was engrossed in study at the library when she heard someone softly speaking her name. "Julie. Julie. Is that really you?" Julie looked up to focus slowly on a familiar face. "Doug, is that you?" she countered in a startled voice. "Yes," Doug answered, enjoying his discovery, "I thought it was you. Do you want to go for coffee and talk like in the old days?" "Sure, why not? I could use a break."

Over coffee and the din of the university cafeteria they caught up with each other's news. Julie thought Doug was at school in San Diego, but here he was in Santa Barbara. He explained that he had been accepted at both places and at the last minute had decided to move north instead of south.

Doug saw great changes in Julie, changes that intrigued him. Julie was surprised at his interest but felt relaxed and safe with her old friend as they took up their relationship where they had left it a year and a half before—casual and unhurried.

During the spring term they had a class together, which gave Doug an opportunity to use homework and projects to circumvent Julie's reserve.

One evening before midterm exams Julie found herself in Doug's dorm room studying. She hadn't realized as they worked that Doug's roommates had gone out. As they broke for coffee Doug put his arm around her, first in a brotherly way and then more affectionately. She nestled closer to him on the couch. As they embraced she slipped slowly down, resting her head on the pillow. Doug lay over her. It felt so good to be in his arms.

He gently caressed her. At first it seemed so natural to be close to Doug, but then a voice inside her bagan to cry, No...no...no. The past overtook the present, and she sat up abruptly, wondering how she could have forgotten so easily. "What's wrong, Julie?" "I can't, Doug. I just can't go on." Julie was unable to say anything else, but their closeness and his touch had triggered feelings from the past, the awful past she could no longer repress.

Julie was so damaged and hurt; yet Doug, not understanding, was hurt too, and very confused. She couldn't talk about it, which perplexed him further, but he knew he cared about her. She was a mystery to him.

Their special romance of caring and distance continued through Doug's graduation and on into the summer. But strangely, when Julie returned to Santa Barbara in the fall she felt relief from Doug's daily presence. They wrote letters, and he visited her in Santa Barbara from time to time. But their romance quieted as Doug began to date women from his office and Julie began her practice teaching. She restored the protective shell around herself. She dated casually but never allowed any serious relationships.

As time passed Julie was surprised to realize that she hadn't thought of her baby in ages. Even his fourth birthday went by unremembered. How could this be, she wondered?

She was feeling freer as she headed toward graduation and her first year of teaching back home, where she felt lucky to have landed a job. Her baby wasn't so much a deep dark secret as it was just a part of her past. She still fantasized about seeing him someday, but he was now seven years old and seemed to be part of another world.

Her first year of teaching, in third grade, was wonderful. Julie was an especially good teacher. She had a sensitivity to children, a special intuitive ability to guide them without resorting to some of the disciplinary measures used by the older teachers. She felt rewarded as she completed her first year and looked forward to summer vacation.

Julie was twenty-four. She felt her life was going the way

she wanted it to. Thoughts of her "baby" were misty in her memory. She pondered her accomplishments and felt pleased that she had reached her goal—but why wasn't she satisfied?

Thoughts of Doug kept tugging at her. She pushed them aside, but again and again she found him on her mind. She hadn't had contact with Doug for so long; why was he popping into her mind now? She had always appreciated the way he had respected her and had not pushed his way into her life. Had she been the one who had turned him away? Gentle, caring Doug—had she? What a mistake! What a loss! It had taken all this time to realize how deeply she cared for him. But instead she had created another loss for herself.

The new realization stayed with Julie and moved her to thoughts of contacting Doug, but fear that he had found someone else made her anxious. Still she knew she must write to him. She hoped he would still be with the pharmaceutical company he had joined four years ago.

Dear Doug,

I can imagine how surprised you are to hear from me after all these years. I've graduated from college and am now teaching at an elementary school in Irvine.

It sure has been a long time. I didn't know where you were, but I took a chance on catching up with you at work. Hope you don't mind. Maybe we could talk over coffee after work someday. If it doesn't work out, I'll understand, but it surely would be fun seeing you again. Hope to hear from you.

Sincerely,
Julie

Julie agonized for a month waiting for a response. Could Doug be married? Had he moved away? Did he want to forget her? The lack of communication tormented her. How could she have been so foolish as not to see the person he was? He probably has a steady girlfriend, she punished herself.

Julie had given up hope of hearing from Doug when his letter arrived with an apology.

Dear Julie,

I'm sorry it's taken so long to respond to your letter. I've been away on a six-week business trip. Sure, coffee sounds great.

I'll meet you at 4:00 on Saturday at the Balboa Pier, and we'll catch up from there.

See you then.
Doug

Julie was overwhelmed with joy at the thought of seeing Doug, but she cautioned herself not to rush ahead. He still could be involved with someone else and just want to touch base with her one last time. The days couldn't pass quickly enough until at last it was Saturday. Julie found herself filled with excitement and anticipation.

She arrived early at the Balboa Pier and watched the bicyclists and roller skaters parade up and down the beachfront walk in the late afternoon sun. Then in the distance a handsome, mature young man approached her. They caught each other's eye and as if hypnotized walked toward one another. They hugged each other for a long time and then laughed away their nervousness over the exuberance of their greeting.

Arm in arm they walked along the beach. The time apart

suddenly seemed like no time at all as first one talked and then the other about their lives.

Doug was settling into his job and being given more and more opportunities. Yes, he had had a steady girlfriend for a couple of years, but they had broken up a year ago. For the last year he had had a number of girlfriends but nothing serious.

Julie talked about her teaching, and the children at school, and how wonderful her life seemed. And then she grew silent. Doug recognized in her the same faraway look he remembered—the look he could never get beyond; the distance he could never cut through. He stopped and sat down on the sand, beckoning Julie to do the same.

"Julie, I see in you the same look that has kept us apart too long. I must know what it is that is troubling you."

Tears welled up in Julie's eyes as she felt she was risking everything by telling Doug about her baby, but somehow she started anyway. She shared the hurt and the love over her lost child—her deep caring about this baby whom she knew she must give up and the grief and emptiness that had haunted her over the years. She had never told anyone for fear of reproach. And she had promised herself she would never tell a boyfriend about her past.

Doug listened patiently. When she fell silent he spoke with feeling. "Julie, the past has been hard on you. Don't punish yourself anymore. What you have been through doesn't change anything for us. Now that I know what you have been through, I love you because of it. From your struggle, your courage and caring, you show me the extent of your ability to love. You are a very special person, and I care for you all the more."

"Doug, you're not upset about my past?" "No, Julie. I respect you for everything you are."

The two sat huddled together on the beach as first a blazing sunset and then dusk overtook them and blended together the past, the present, and the future for Julie and Doug.

CHAPTER 18

Time Passes: Darlene

Unlike some of my former students, Darlene kept in touch over the years. At first I'd hear from her every few months. Later it would be once a year, and finally years would roll by between our visits. I came to know that when Darlene had a need, she either came by the school or telephoned me to talk.

When Darlene's time at S.A.M. ended, I still was greatly concerned about her. I had taken as many opportunities as I could to help her understand what her responsibilities would be, but I doubted how effective my efforts would prove to be. Her unwillingness to change was frustrating, and I worried about her, her baby Shannon, and her rocky marriage to Bob.

A "Bandaid approach" to life was Grace's term for Darlene's shortsighted, short-term, superficial way of solving problems. We both wondered what lay ahead for her.

It wasn't long before Darlene stormed into school early one morning. "I'm mad as hell," she broke out. "Bob really pisses me off. We had this big fight last night. He pushed me around a little, but I showed him. I hit him with an ashtray. Before I knew it, blood was streaming down his face. I sure got even with him. He went out for a while, so I thought I'd go over and visit my girlfriends. I had to talk to someone. When I came back, all his stuff was gone. He had the nerve to move out! What am I supposed to do? I guess he's just good for nothing like his father."

The girls at S.A.M. couldn't help but become involved with Darlene's tirade. First one and then another offered solutions for her. "You can go down to the Department of Social Service and get on welfare. If you have a baby and no way to support it, they'll give you welfare. You just sign up, and you'll get a check every month." With this information Darlene was somewhat relieved and decided to try getting welfare.

Months went by before we heard from Darlene again. This time she told about her divorce and being thrown out of her apartment because she hadn't paid the rent. How was she supposed to pay the rent when "the stupid welfare check isn't enough to live on!" I suggested that she move in with her Mom or Dad. "Oh hell, not them. I can't stand them—that's why I moved out in the first place." She thought for a moment. "But Dad does have a spare bedroom. I guess me 'n Shannon could stay there for a while. He's got a new wife and she's a bitch. I hope I can stand her."

"You only have to stay there untill you get a job. There is a job training program that provides day care. You can go there and learn a skill for a job that will pay you more than welfare," I encouraged.

It was obvious that my "job" idea wasn't of interest to Darlene, but at least she had more options for herself and could make choices, whether they were conscious choices or not.

Darlene did move in with her father, and they got along fairly well. But in time friction developed between Darlene and her stepmother. What with Darlene's habits, Shannon's crying, the stepmother's resentment, and her father's temper, Darlene decided she would have to move. She arranged to join some girlfriends who had a crowded apartment in central Costa Mesa.

I hadn't held out much hope for my job training idea, but I continued to encourage Darlene to begin it. She said she might be able to start after she had moved.

Shannon was now a year old as Darlene dragged her and their belongings over to the two-bedroom apartment. The girls were in and out at all hours of the day and night, so they weren't concerned about Darlene's and Shannon's moving in. It meant one more welfare check to help pay the rent. Darlene saw it as an opportunity to have baby-sitters to give her more free time. Little Shannon had a disturbing look about her as the experiences of her one short year of life wore away the innocent expression I'd remembered. Her demeanor turned to grasping demands for meeting the basic needs of life.

Darlene commented that Shannon was so demanding all the time. She was impossible to be with. She had a temper that she got from her father. But living at the apartment allowed Darlene to get away and leave Shannon with the girls. Darlene liked that.

The apartment was no place for a child. Aside from the filth, the people who wandered in and out were into drugs. To them this going-on-two-year-old was a nuisance who always seemed to need something to shut her up.

One Saturday morning Darlene decided to go to the swap meet at the fairgrounds, and she asked her roommates to keep an eye on Shannon. At the swap meet she met Pete, who was selling old household items. Darlene hung around the stall where he hawked his wares accompanied by a humorous patter. Pete was a suntanned blond of about twenty-five whose biceps bulged out of his tight T-shirt. Darlene was attracted to him and flirted with him as she learned that he liked to have a good time and wasn't attached to anyone. The more she hung around, the more he let her hype the customers, and the more fun they had.

Darlene could hardly believe how the time had flown by. It seemed as if she had just got there when Pete began packing up for the day. He said he'd see her around and took off. Darlene decided to come back and spend Sunday with him.

When she got back to the apartment she could hear Shannon screaming. Going in, she found Shannon huddled under the kitchen sink—red-faced, sweaty, and dirty. Her roommates weren't home. Darlene was really angry. How could they just go out and leave Shannon alone? She tried to quiet Shannon, but the child was hysterical. The incessant crying made Darlene angrier. She found a baby bottle, filled it with juice, and jammed it in the baby's mouth as she laid her on the couch. Shannon acted as if she hadn't eaten all day as she desperately sucked the bottle dry and then fell into a deep sleep.

Darlene felt trapped. She couldn't even go out without something happening. Besides, how was she going to get back to the swap meet to see Pete again? She left the sleeping Shannon and went upstairs to the apartment of an older woman to ask her to baby-sit Shannon the next day. The woman asked if the baby was all right and said she'd heard her crying a lot earlier in the day. Darlene explained it away, and the woman agreed to baby-sit. Darlene breathed a sigh a relief.

That night when her roommates returned, Darlene let them have it with a barrage of cuss words about how they'd left Shannon all day, hadn't fed or changed her, and how Shannon was screaming her head off when Darlene returned. They blankly said they understood Darlene to say she wouldn't be long. They weren't at fault for leaving; *she* was at fault for not coming home. The argument raged on and on with Shannon sleeping through the din, the victim of it all.

The next day Darlene took Shannon upstairs to the sitter and raced off to the swap meet to look for Pete.

The woman cuddled and tried to comfort this wild, desperate child as best she could. She bathed Shannon, washed her matted hair, and tended to the diaper rash. How could a mother abuse a child with such neglect, she wondered? Worry about this uncared-for child and neglectful mother prompted her to call the authorities and report Darlene. She had seen child neglect before and done nothing about it, but she knew this abuse would continue, and her heart wouldn't let the child go through it without someone on her side. She was fearful of what Darlene might do, so she determined to deny everything if Darlene questioned her.

Meanwhile at the swap meet Darlene found Pete, and the two of them hawked the wares to the crowds of people passing by, and all the while became physically intrigued with each other.

The next time I heard from Darlene she was angry again and wanted me to know all about it. Shannon had been taken away by the police because some "asshole" thought she wan't a good enough mother. She was going to find out who had reported her and get even! Now she couldn't get Shannon back until she found a decent home for her. She and Pete were seeing a great deal of each other, and Darlene hoped it would work out for her to move into his place.

Pete had a fairly good job as a helper with a moving and storage company. He was enterprising and arranged with customers to remove any discarded items free of charge. It was amazing what he talked people into leaving behind. They found it easier to let him haul their discards away than to deal with them themselves. It was these items that Pete sold at the swap meet, making a "few bucks" on the side.

Darlene did move into Pete's place. Pete wasn't interested in being tied down. He just liked having someone to share his bed. But Darlene vowed to get her baby back and went about making the place good enough to pass the inspection of the social service workers who would be "putting their noses into her business." Darlene did get her baby back, and life smoothed out for a while.

The next time I saw Darlene she was showing off her newborn baby, Tamara. "Her daddy is really proud of her," Darlene said. "Pete and I've been doin' OK. We're not at the apartment anymore. Pete got a good deal renting a room at the Camelot Motel behind the gas station on Harbor Boulevard. It's got a small kitchen with a hot plate and refrigerator," Darlene said defensively. "Shannon likes it. Don't you, honey?" Four-year-old Shannon looked up from pulling books out of the bookcase in the S.A.M. office. "Uh huh," she grunted, not really hearing what her mother had said. The dark circles under Shannon's eyes bothered me, but I could see no marks of physical abuse.

Darlene said how happy she was with Pete, and how he had got used to the idea of being a father, especially now that little Tamara was born. My concern for this family overwhelmed me. First Shannon, now Tamara. Where were the solutions for these tangled destinies?

Three years passed without a visit from Darlene. I hoped the lack of contact meant things were going along all right. My yearly enrollment of new students kept me focused on new and immediate needs. It was only when a newspaper article about a lost child came to my attention that I realized that the three-year-old Tamara described was Darlene's daughter. Tamara had wandered off and was found the next morning sleeping in a box she had been playing in behind the supermarket five blocks from home.

Darlene came to school to tell us all about her ordeal, enjoying the attention of the girls as she described her sleepless night worrying about Tamara.

Darlene said that Pete had taken off about a year ago and that she had been living with her mother until she met Dave, a guy she liked who was a cook in a restaurant. Dave knew of a well-paying job in Las Vegas, and he was leaving next week. She thought she'd take the kids and go with him, especially because she thought she was pregnant again. She hoped he would marry her and things would straighten out.

Then years went by and I heard nothing from Darlene until one day an old dented '75 Chevy limped into our parking lot, and Darlene got out with her three kids, Jeremy, four, Tamara, seven, and Shannon, eleven. Darlene looked thin. Her coarse face was covered with heavy makeup. The unwashed children were unruly as they sneered at and pushed one another. Only the restraint of being in a strange place kept them from fighting.

"Oh God," Darlene began, "that bastard Dave started going out with chicks in Las Vegas, and I couldn't stand it. I had to get out of there. We've been here a couple of weeks and can't find anywhere to stay. Mom and Dad are gone. I don't have any money. We've been living in Santa Ana canyon in the car."

I fed them with what we had at S.A.M. and gave them food to take with them. I called the Interfaith Shelter, where they could stay up to sixty days, but after that it was up to them. What a frustration Darlene was to me. Surely now she would take some responsibility for herself and stop blaming others for her misfortunes. She was twenty-eight years old. I wondered what circumstances, what pain, what combination of conditions it would take for Darlene to wake up and stop letting life happen to her. Her life was like a rock lyric with the same words repeating themselves over and over again.

Shannon was fourteen when Darlene called to talk again. "I can't believe it," she began. "You won't believe it either, Mrs. Whitfield. It's about Shannon—she's pregnant! I know I'm not perfect, and I haven't had money, but if I'd been given a chance things might have turned out different. I'm just so shocked about Shannon, but I know it's not my fault. It's Shannon's fault. She should have known better . . ."

CHAPTER 19

Time Passes: Joe

I didn't have personal contact with Joe and Rita through the years, but Rita's younger sister, Mariella, became a S.A.M. student, and through her I kept up with the current affairs of Joe and Rita.

Mariella and Rita were very close, and often at vacation times Mariella went by bus to visit her.

Joe and Rita lived in the central California town of Salinas, where they shared an apartment with Joe's cousin and his wife. When Joe first joined Rita there, he searched for a job. Joe's cousin worked in the fields picking lettuce and other crops. Joe hired on with the crew, and each day they rode in the back of a truck to the farms in the valley to earn what they could. It was hard work, and at the end of the first week Joe's back was so sore he could hardly straighten up. His hand was cut in several places from the blade he used to strip the lettuce from the ground. The more crates he filled, the more he earned. Joe wondered at the end of the second week if he could even continue. He vowed he would get out of farm work as soon as he could. He enrolled in adult night school and worked to earn a high school diploma. He was good at setting his sights on what he wanted.

Joe and Rita were happy at being together. They loved and enjoyed little Joseph, and their life seemed to be working out according to their plans.

The first year passed with Joe working in the fields and going to school at night. By the end of summer he received his diploma. Rita attended the Salinas School Age Mother program with little Joseph, and she too graduated from high school.

Another couple moved into the apartment, which made it cheaper but much more cramped in space. The relief from some of the monthly payment made up for the discomfort and enabled this financially shaky family to have a few more dollars each month, giving Rita a greater sense of security.

The main argument between Joe and Rita was over money. She felt he spent money foolishly, such as buying unneeded things for Joseph and things for a car they didn't even have. She thought she could manage their money much better than he could.

Joe couldn't wait for Rita to turn eighteen so they could be married without needing Rita's parents' permission. Sure enough, the marriage finally took place, and Rita's sister told me how beautiful the wedding was.

They were married by the priest in the Catholic church. Even though the wedding dresses were borrowed, everyone looked beautiful, Mariella said. Rita's white lace veil draped softly over her long black hair, around her face and shoulders, and down her back to the hem of her dress. Joe was overcome at the sight of her, and his eyes filled with tears of emotion. Mariella still looked starry-eyed as she described it. Little Joseph was dressed in a new outfit Joe had bought for him.

Afterward the small wedding party returned to the apartment, where they celebrated with wedding cake, beer, and a special bottle of champagne Joe's cousin had purchased. They laughed the evening away. Joe and Rita sneaked off to their room for their own private chance to express their commitment and love to one another.

During the second year Rita became pregnant again, and Joe determined to get out of migrant field work. When he learned of an opening at the sugar beet processing plant, he applied and was taken on in the shipping dock, loading trucks with cases of sugar headed for distribution across the country. One would have thought this new job and the chance to make good money would have freed Joe and Rita from their arguments about money. Quite the contrary, the more money Joe made, the more he spent on things that Rita felt were silly. Joe also joined the baseball team sponsored by the plant. After the games or practices, Joe sat with the other guys on the hoods of their cars drinking beer, talking, and—according to Rita—looking and acting macho. She didn't like his spending time and money that way when they had a baby coming and needed to save. What if something happened? Rita worried that they would never get out on their own at this rate. The crowded apartment wasn't going to be their way of life forever, Rita vowed.

Their arguments didn't seem to get anywhere. Joe had his way and Rita had hers. Joe had learned from his father that the man rules the family and the woman takes care of the house. Rita argued that it didn't matter what Joe's father thought or did, she and Joe had no money because Joe was spending it all as *he* pleased. What they needed to do was figure out how to spend the money so they *all* were better off.

Although Joe didn't like Rita's making a stand against him and his way of doing things, he eventually agreed to put away a part of his paycheck each week. The new baby would be here soon, and more money would be needed for bills—that was certain. Why make it harder on Rita by holding out when a small sacrifice on his part would make things better all around?

Baby Maria looked adorable in her long white christening gown. The whole family came up from southern California to be at the church with Joe and Rita on this special day. Joe and Rita were nervous about seeing Rita's parents again. They hoped that time would have healed the rift between them. Surely the new baby would soften the sharp edges of their differences. And it proved to be just that way.

When Maria was two and Joseph was four, Joe decided to move his family out of the apartment. He was making more money, and they could afford to have more room. Rita wanted to work part time and became involved with a woman who showed her how to sell Tupperware. It worked out well, so Rita thought, as Joe could stay home and take care of the kids and she got a chance not only to make extra money but to do something different. Job traded off his reluctance at having Rita away from home when the extra money mounted up and it looked as if they might be able to afford a car.

The car became a reality, and Joe added to it all the things he'd collected through the years, making it just the way he wanted it. Every Sunday, like a ritual, Joe proudly drove his family to the park for his baseball game. When baseball season was over, it was soccer. After a while Rita began to resent so much of Joe's time being spent at midweek practice or at the games. One evening after practice Joe went out with the team for a few beers. He was later than usual getting home, and Rita had reached the breaking point. When he came in a little drunk, she exploded in a rush of angry words. Joe fought back with words he might not have said if it hadn't been for the beers. The children were scared and started to cry. Joe defended his need to be with the guys, and Rita defended her need for him to spend more time at home with her and the children. They couldn't seem to resolve the problem.

For the next weeks they picked at each other. Joe went off to the next two Sunday games with things still not settled. Finally Rita began to realize how much Joe's sports meant to him, and it was she who decided that they needed to talk about it. Joe silently was relieved when Rita opened the conversation. Their anger had cooled, and now they could talk. Rita acknowledged Joe's desire to play baseball, and Joe tried to understand Rita's frustration over the time his sports took him away from her and the children. They both began to realize that what they had together was what really counted. If that meant Joe's continuing baseball, then Rita decided she could live with it, and she told him so. Afterward, they hugged each other, glad to have things worked out once more.

The children, now in school, grew under the guidance and spirit of Joe and Rita. They felt loved and respected. The family with its well-kept secondhand car and small apartment had few of the material things that are viewed as indications of success. But Joe and Rita were wealthy and successful in so many nonmaterial ways. They learned that in life you don't lose by being second.

Joe liked his job, and because he did well, he earned advancements and made more money. He had been at the sugar beet factory for ten years, but it didn't seem that long. Each day Rita packed a lunch for him, and each noon Joe and the guys sat together under a big tree eating and swapping stories. A group of women sometimes gathered nearby. One woman in particular Joe kept noticing. She always wore a short skirt or tight pants with a low-cut blouse. Rita never dressed like that, he thought. This woman always seemed to have a touch of lace showing in just the places where he wanted to see it. Sometimes when she leaned forward he could see the contour of her breasts. She excited fantasies in him. Her full black hair, flashing dark eyes, and gold hoop earrings held his attention.

Sometimes this woman, Teresa, walked out with him and talked for a while before each joined their friends for lunch. Their talks became more involved until finally Teresa began bringing Joe special desserts she had prepared for him. It was all innocent, Joe believed, because they were with everyone. Nothing was secretive.

One afternoon Teresa's car broke down, and she asked Joe if he would take her home. Joe didn't mind. He loved showing off his car, which was painted a flashy color and had all new upholstery. When they arrived at Teresa's apartment she invited him in, but Joe felt awkward and went on home, saying nothing to Rita about Teresa.

Teresa was attracted to Joe. She was young and unmarried and had a special way with men. She usually got what she wanted, and she wanted Joe. Teresa looked for an opportunity to be alone with Joe.

The Salinas rodeo was a week away. Joe's baseball game conflicted with the big parade. Although he wanted to go with Rita and the kids to see the parade and the horses at the fairgrounds afterward, the game was an important one and he didn't want to miss it. Rita would be gone all day with the children. She didn't mind missing the ball game but was disappointed that Joe couldn't be with her. They compromised that Joe would try to find them at the fairgrounds after the parade.

Rita and the kids went off to the parade, and Joe to his game. During the game Joe noticed Teresa in the stands. What was she doing at the ball game, he wondered? Afterward Teresa came over and explained that she needed help with her car, which was back at her apartment. Her roommate had driven her over to the park. It was her last resort. He was the only one she could think of who could help her. The rest of the team went off for their usual beer, leaving Joe behind with Teresa.

Joe drove her home, but he was feeling strange; pictures of Rita and the kids kept popping into his head. What was the matter with him? He wasn't going to jeopardize anything by taking Teresa home and fixing her car for her! When he got the loose battery cable fixed and the car started, Teresa offered him a beer, and they went into her apartment. They talked there for some time. Teresa explained that her roommate had gone to the rodeo. Joe, softened by the beer, the scent of her perfume, and the willingness of her body, found himself unable to resist the inevitable plan that Teresa had set out to fulfill. Rightness or wrongness disappeared into instinctive desire.

Rita and the children looked in vain for Joe at the fairgrounds. They boarded the bus for the ride home. There they found Joe, watching TV. He said he was tired so he came home. Rita was perplexed but didn't pursue the issue. She went to the kitchen to prepare dinner. The children told their dad all about the parade and the horses, and did most of the talking. Joe was quiet, and Rita was puzzled.

When dinner was over and the children were in bed, Rita asked if anything were wrong. Just tired, Joe explained.

Weeks went by. Although Joe felt he was acting normally, Rita sensed something wrong. Then at a Sunday game when Rita was sitting with some of the other wives, one mentioned the name Teresa as a girl who suddenly seemed to have a particular interest in their baseball team. She now attended all the games. It was all Rita needed to set her thinking. She asked if Teresa had been at the game the Sunday of the rodeo. Rita could see from the sudden change of expression that the woman felt she had said too much already.

Rita received this news with a piercing stab of pain. Somehow she had to find out what this was all about. Was Joe involved? She would see what she could find out that night from Joe.

When he got home, Rita confronted him. What was this about Teresa? Why was she at the game? Where did you go with her? Rita's barrage was unmerciful. Joe became defensive. He wouldn't admit anything. Rita felt that meant he was guilty, and she told him he had disgraced her and the children. The argument accelerated to the point that Joe picked up some clothes, stuffed them in a bag, and left in a rage.

For a week Joe stayed with his cousin. He felt defensive and didn't want any part of Rita's harassment. Another week went by.

Rita was heartbroken. She cried herself to sleep at night. Here was everything they had worked so hard for—shattered, ruined. How could this have happened? She wanted to believe; now how could she ever believe again? She had always been faithful and assumed he would be too.

Joe was angry. He didn't care about Teresa. He didn't want her anyway. He knew that what he and Teresa had done was wrong, but he felt caught. Teresa was a bad mistake. He didn't mean for it to be anything. It just happened. Teresa didn't change his honest love for Rita. Joe's anger kept him from coming back to Rita.

As the weeks went by, Rita softened. Her Joe would

always be her Joe. She longed for the affection of the old days. Joe had always been so gentle and caring. She missed him and wanted him back.

Rita called Joe at his cousin's apartment and tearfully asked him to come home. He brought his things back and sat down in their living room again. The kids hugged him and playfully tugged at him, but the pressures of the last weeks kept him from letting down as he went through the motions of their greeting.

Although he was home, the tension of what might be ahead got in the way of any final reconciliation. Rita wondered if she could ever trust again, and Joe wondered if he could be forgiven. In each there was a desire to have things the way they were before, but they wondered how long it would take.

Six months passed as the marriage tried to right itself. First Rita and then Joe did things to indicate their love and willingness to work things out. The time of separation showed them that what they had together was far better than being apart. They shared the same commitment to their children and their family. Grudges were never a part of their relationship. The realization for both came at almost the same moment, with the words, "I forgive you, Joe...I'm sorry, Rita."

Joe and Rita weren't going to ruin their lives over this. They had the love, faith, and ability to resolve their differences. The struggles of the past had helped build an even stronger respect and caring between them in their renewed life together.

When Mariella told me this story, I couldn't help remembering Joe and Rita fifteen years before at S.A.M. and "...the power of their love and the spirit they showed in finding a way to work things out."

CHAPTER 20

And then...

The true influence of S.A.M. we may never know. Only in the final reckoning will the full meaning be known and perhaps understood.

It is our hope that students gain a new insight, a feeling of self-worth, an educational advantage, so that in turn these S.A.M. mothers may influence their children in a positive way.

But teachers' hopes are not always realities. Alexandria was brought back in thought to S.A.M. by words that she remembered at a time when she needed them most.

Fragile Cecille needed to return to S.A.M. to complete unfinished business so she could be at peace.

Julie appreciated our acceptance and support, but she gave much to us.

Darlene was our frustration.

We might never have known about Joe and Rita except by chance.

The lives shared in this book are the realities of teenage pregnancy. These stories are the bottom line, and they continue to be as the young face the problem of teenage pregnancy at S.A.M.'s door.

What can be done to prevent the apparent inevitability of teenage pregnancies? We know that they result from ignorance, immaturity, visual and printed media pressures, unresolved needs, peer pressures, and cultural pressures. The vulnerable girl or boy is caught in the gap between physical maturity and emotional maturity.

The causes that shape the thinking of young people need to be addressed forthrightly with conviction and knowledge.

In many cases, mothers and fathers, religious leaders, teachers, and community leaders have relinquished their right and authority to address the problem, and teen age pregnancy continues to be the result.

Who will take up the challenge?